SPOTTED DICK,
s'il vous plaît

SPOTTED DICK,
s'il vous plaît

An English Restaurant
in France

Tom Higgins

First published in Great Britain by Aurum Press Limited in 1994
under the title *Plat du Jour: An English Restaurant in Lyons*

Published by
Soho Press Inc.
853 Broadway
New York, NY 10003

Library of Congress Cataloging-in-Publication Data

Higgins, Tom, 1954–
Spotted Dick, s'il vous plait: an English restaurant in France/
Tom Higgins.
p.   cm.
ISBN 1–56947–032–4
1. Restaurants—France—Lyon. I. Title.
TX910.F8H54   1995
641.5′09445′823—dc20   94-43484
                                                 CIP

To June

SPOTTED DICK,
s'il vous plaît

1

Lugdunum, ancient capital of Gaul, Roman town, medieval centre of culture, city of science, learning, medicine and theology . . . Lyon has many claims to fame. And yet, have people chosen to remember Lyon for scientific advances, philosophical ideas, art or literature? No, they haven't. They have chosen to remember Lyon for its cooking and for its restaurants. All over France, Lyon is regarded as a kind of gastronomic paradise where the art of presenting food at table has been carried to unheard-of heights. 'You're going to Lyon, are you? *Vous allez très bien manger,*' say the French. And the fact is, it's true: Lyon does have a tremendous restaurant tradition. Generations of Lyonnais, growing up in the midst of a multitude of restaurants, have a very clear picture of what a restaurant should be like, and this is something I suppose I should have thought about before launching myself on their gastronomic ocean. What could an Englishman possibly have to add to the Lyonnais restaurant world? What could he show the French about running a restaurant – an almost archetypally French trade? Was there even the smallest gap in the market for him to fill? Well, I'm afraid I considered none of these questions when I opened my restaurant in Lyon, since for me it was the realization of a dream, and dreams, when they come within reach, have a tendency to override reason.

Quite honestly, if there is one thing that the city of Lyon does not need, then that is another restaurant. It already has thousands of restaurants. In every street there are cafés, bistros, bars, brasseries and other sorts of eating establishments. You would be hard put to find a single street in the town which is without some kind of restaurant. In certain, self-appointed gastronomic corners, there is almost nothing else – whole streets are lined with them. It would be possible to compose an olfactory guide to the town, with visitors finding their way around the streets during the restaurant preparation hours by literally following their noses: 'Starting on the Place des Jacobins, raise your head towards the south-west and wait until the mingled scents of saffron and paprika come wafting towards you, leading you to where Christian Bourrillot is preparing his famous speciality, then let the pungent aroma of glazed onions lead you eastwards' and so on. There are restaurants offering specialities from all corners of the globe: Chinese restaurants, Indian restaurants, Malaysian restaurants, Mexican restaurants; Thai-food restaurants, Spanish, Italian and Portuguese restaurants; Brazilian restaurants, Norwegian and Russian restaurants. Then there are restaurants specializing in the cuisine from all the regions of France: Basque restaurants, Périgord restaurants, Savoyard restaurants; restaurants with specialities from Brittany, Normandy and the Midi, not to mention, of course, innumerable Lyonnais restaurants.

Much has been written about French cooking, many books published about the multitude of different styles in the various regions of France. I do not think I would be exaggerating, however, in saying that the Rhône Alpes region, with Lyon at its centre, is the area most renowned for fine cuisine. Lyon certainly considers itself to be the gastronomic capital of France, possibly of the world. There is, around Lyon, an extremely high concentration of Michelin three-star restaurants. From these, down to the humblest of bistros, there are countless establishments serving excellent food for prices lower than elsewhere. I do not believe there is another place like Lyon in Europe: there are chefs here who are sacrificing themselves on the altar of food in order to serve better and better dishes at more and more reasonable prices. Come here quickly, while it lasts. Something will have to snap soon.

'*Les Lyonnais aiment bien manger*' – the Lyonnais are a good restaurant clientele; they love to go out to eat. And yet, I cannot help wondering if there are not rather too many restaurants in Lyon. Sometimes I wonder if everybody in the town – every single man-jack among them – went out to a restaurant, whether every seat in every restaurant would be filled, or whether there would still be some empty places.

The Lyonnais love to eat, but they do not love to pay very much for their food – restaurants are cheaper in Lyon than in any other French town that I know. Here, in the capital of gastronomy, to run a restaurant is a vocation, a genuine calling requiring absolute devotion. But to turn what amounts to a spiritual journey of the soul into a money-making concern is far from simple. New restaurants open only to go bankrupt with monotonous regularity

Given this situation, was it wise, I wonder, to open a restaurant in a back street of an old-fashioned area of town, filled with bars serving cheap lunchtime menus, where the *petits vieux* still line up at eight in the morning to drink their glasses of white wine, cognac or *gno circle*? Was it wise, did it show sound commercial sense to name this restaurant 'Mister Higgins', and to launch an onslaught on French gastronomy by means of a cuisine – the British – which the French consider to be next to inedible?

Of course it wasn't wise, but at the time the question of wisdom did not really come into it. I simply wanted a restaurant, had one within my grasp, and did not stop to think of all the countless more experienced restaurateurs who had been forced to close their businesses. I did not think about the out-of-the-way location of the restaurant, I did not concern myself with how difficult it is to park in our area of town at night, or how the French love to drive and hate to walk. I was not even wholly aware of quite how strongly the French feel about English cooking. Now, eight years later, I have a very clear picture of the French vision of our national cuisine: I have had their views expressed to me in innumerable ways. Once I was sitting in the restaurant at lunchtime on a day when it was closed. A group of five or six people walked down the street.

'*Tiens,*' said one, '*voilá le restaurant anglais.*'

'*Y'a pas grand-monde,*' said another. '*En fait, pas un chat.*'

'*C'est normal,*' said a third. '*C'est á cause de l'horreur du pudding anglais.*' And off they went, laughing uproariously at their terrific wit, not for a moment thinking that the restaurant was in fact empty simply because it was closed, and not because of the horror of the English pudding. On another occasion, a couple turned up at the restaurant and had to be refused because we were full. The woman was furious: '*Mon dieu!*' she cursed, '*un restau anglais á Lyon, et il faut retenir!*' What was the world coming to when you had to reserve to get a seat in a restaurant which was clearly little more than a joke?

But in order to understand properly the French attitude to British food it must be remembered that the French consider their cuisine to be at the very summit of culinary art. No other national cuisine equals theirs, and the only one which is really worthy of consideration is, no, not the Italian, but the Chinese. That can at least be taken seriously. From the vertiginous heights of culinary genius, the French are able to look down, perhaps a little complacently, at the levels below. Somewhere very near the bottom indeed lies British cooking, perhaps jostling for bottom place with German and Austrian cooking.

Now a French person knows about cooking. It is part of his national heritage. Even as children in kindergarten, the French are already eating three-course meals starting with mixed salads, continuing with meat or fish and ending up with *fromage blanc* or dessert. Food is advertised everywhere. Newspapers, magazines, television, the cinema, news hoardings (of which there are too many, littered about the countryside), free advertising pamphlets (there are far too many of these too), all contain advertisements of people shovelling large quantities of food or drink into their mouths – beautiful, young, principally female people, tucking into cakes, cheese, yoghurt, chocolate, creams, pâtés, meat, fish, terrines, starters, main courses, desserts, snacks, bread, croissants, wine, beer, aperitifs, whisky, gin, vodka. With all these images around, it's a wonder that people eat anything at all. Especially as the stuff advertised tends, as it does everywhere, to be the most instant, artificial food imaginable.

Anyway the French know all about cooking, and what they know about British cooking is this: it is awful. We take legs of perfectly good lamb and boil them furiously into grey, pulpy messes. The same treatment is handed out to our vegatables. We eat jam with our meat. In fact, we make a point of mixing *sucré* with *salé*, to the extent that it is impossible to eat any savoury dish in Britain without a good dollop of sweet sauce. One customer once assured me that when on exile in Britain to conquer the language in two weeks, she had eaten a *'poulet á la marmelade'*. Did we ever serve such a thing in our restaurant? Our puddings are allowed to be good, as are our biscuits and sweets. The English breakfast is appreciated, but if there is one thing we have invented which for sheer repulsiveness tops all the other horrors we perpetrate in our kitchens, it is jelly. The

French have a deepseated, almost pathological fear of jelly. Many of them have stories of mothers of families where they lodged as teenagers (still trying to learn English), producing a particularly grotesque green, red, orange or yellow jelly, which sat quivering on the table in front of them in all its ghastliness. I believe that jelly has cost me a lot of customers: people refuse to try my restaurant, because they believe that it will be impossible for them to get out of the door without eating at least a couple of mouthfuls of this terrible stuff – 'Come along now, ONE for Mummy and ONE for Daddy . . .'

In an effort to conquer this fear of jellies, I sold them under the name of *terrines de fruits*. I filled a mould with carefully pared slices of orange, and another with hulled strawberries, then poured over a home-made fruit jelly mixture, containing just enough gelatine to hold the fruit in slices when cut. I would serve one slice of strawberry terrine and one slice of orange terrine. Round the strawberry slice would go a circle of custard, round the orange slice a circle of raspberry coulis. Whole strawberries cut into fans, circles of kiwi fruit, fresh mint leaves were dotted about artistically as garnish. The effect was heartbreakingly beautiful and, I suppose, not very English. All went well unless the customers realized they were eating jelly, then suddenly they could no longer finish.

Nowadays, customers in the restaurant are prepared to admit that the food is good, but do not actually believe that it is British. The French are taught to think very literally in their schools, using the patterns of logic laid out by Descartes. '*C'était très bon,*' people say to me, '*mais pas très anglais.*' Their reasoning goes something like this: All English cooking is bad. This cooking is not bad, therefore it cannot be English. Alain Ville, a friend of ours, had the last word on our enterprise. Once, talking to him, I commented that all his other friends were certifiable maniacs (quite true).

'We', I continued, 'are the only normal friends you have.'

'Yes', he replied, 'you are right. And you have opened an English restaurant in Lyon.'

But then, what were the alternatives? Had I stayed in Britain, I would almost certainly have lived in London. There, it would have been very difficult, not to say impossible, for me to open a restaurant, since high property values, leases, rents and so on, make restaurants very expensive to purchase. Then, quite frankly, the safety and health regulations are almost impossible to meet if you are a small-scale operation. Even if you have only thirty seats, you still have to install a bewildering number of toilets. Surely in these modern times, men and women would be prepared to share one set of toilet facilities? Or does each sex practise arcane rites in the loo which it wishes to keep secret from the other? And just think – the sum of money needed to buy a small terraced house in the centre of London would buy a castle in France, or four Burgundian farmhouses.

I'm not suggesting that everyone should sell their houses and move to Burgundy – there wouldn't be much for them to do there. But somewhere there is a major divergence of values. Compare for a moment the lunch-hour in France and Britain. In France you can eat in an old bistro, the floor of worn red and white tiles, the bar of polished wood with a zinc counter. White paper covers wood tables, faded green leather banquettes line the walls, the chairs are bentwood. Gleaming brass rails run along the tops of the table divisions. Waiters in fusty black waistcoats and long white aprons bustle between the tables. Is this what a restaurant should look like? Or should it have fishing nets hanging from the ceiling, with a catch of bright red plastic lobsters? In England, lunch is likely to be a dismal affair taken in a café (rich in plastic), a fastfood outlet (rich in cardboard), a pub (rich in noise and smoke) or a poor quality Italian restaurant (rich in giant pepper-mills). Well, you may say, lunch is not so important. After all, it's only food, only fuel. Of course, this is true: but here is one of the essential differences between the French and the British. The French do not believe that food is *only* food. One of the things that makes France so attractive is the attention the French pay to the art of everyday life, to the enjoyment of details. A French person would never drink the mixture of coffee powder and water flavoured with milk and sugar that so often passes for breakfast in Britain. In France, drinking coffee is not simply a necessary act to absorb the stimulant required to get the body in motion. The body French requires that the act of drinking coffee should be enjoyable. Hence those beautiful green and gold coffee cups, the freshly ground coffee, the jugs of hot milk, the golden croissants and rounded brioches. What other nation could take bread and chocolate and turn it into *pain au chocolat*? In what other nation would parents allow, indeed encourage, the children to eat bread and chocolate for breakfast?

A recent experience at Heathrow Airport illustrates the same point. Queuing up at a counter for coffee, I noticed as I came nearer to being served that the bar offered 'cappuccinos' at, I think, £1.50 I ordered two. The 'Skyways Coffee Lounge' version of cappuccino was as follows: Take a mug and fill it three-quarters full with a hot black fluid by opening a valve at the bottom of a large, shiny urn. Next, add some cold UHT milk, changing the colour of the fluid to a murky brown. Then take an aerosol can of prewhipped cream and squirt some of it on top of the drink. Finally, sprinkle a spoonful of chocolate chips on to the cream and get the drink to the customer pretty snappishly, since the chocolate falls through the cream very quickly, to become a muddy residue at the bottom of the mug. It is not for nothing, I reflected, as I boarded my flight to France, that the British have adopted the two French expressions *savoir-faire* and *savoir-vivre*; no adequate translation in English exists.

What, then, led us to perpetrate this act of silliness? What possible excuse could we have for such irrational behaviour? Time and again in the restaurant, friendly customers have asked me how I ended up in this city and over the years I have evolved a number of replies. Yet my replies have always dealt with the question of coming to Lyon and very rarely with the question of opening a restaurant, let alone an English restaurant. I suppose that the first question is relatively straightforward. From 1982 to 1986 I worked as a translator, based mainly in Geneva, where I had received part of my education. My wife, Sue, was finishing her training as a doctor. As my employment was on the basis of part-time contracts, I was able to return to Britain fairly regularly, in between conferences, and catch up with my wife, wherever she was working. We even managed to have a child: Harold Xavier Higgins. Now, the object of being married is to live together, and with me in Geneva and Sue in Britain, not a lot of living together was going on. Since Switzerland does not recognize British medical qualifications and Sue did not want to study for another six years to retake Swiss diplomas, practising in that country was clearly not possible. It became clear that we needed a town that was near to Geneva for me, had an international airport (also for me, since my work took me to other countries), and was in the EC, where Sue's medical degree was recognized. If that town were a major hospital centre, so much the better. Lyon was the only choice. At the same time, our friend Alain Ville was leaving his house in Lyon and that was the house we took over.

One matter which had escaped our attention, or which the lure of setting up house in France caused us to ignore, was the fact that in France, the language spoken is French. Sue, possessor of an honest British education, had the wideranging knowledge of that tongue which is the result of many years of study culminating in the securing of a GCE 'O' level qualification. She scarcely spoke a word. This, coupled with a four-month-old child, made the idea of employment as a doctor out of the question. I was working more and more regularly at conferences throughout Europe, and seeing less and less of my family, and besides, translation was beginning to pall – take a look at some of the recommendations issued by the European Commission and you will understand why. Another solution was therefore sought.

One night, some friends had come to dinner. We had just finished eating 'meatloaf wrapped in pastry' – an altogether delicious dish, even if the name is somewhat prosaic. To the French of course, the dish has an exotic appeal not immediately apparent to British people.

'You know,' they said, 'you should open a restaurant; you could serve things like this.'

'Oh yes,' we laughed, taking the remark in the light-hearted spirit in which it was intended, 'we could open a restaurant.'

'You could put it here', they continued, indicating the ground floor of our house with a broad sweep of the arm. Meatloaf was off on the start of a glorious career.

I was not, in fact, entirely innocent in the matter of restaurants. I had worked in two before, as a waiter and as a cook. Both of these were vegetarian cooperatives and although we tried hard and sometimes served quite honourable food, there was an exceptionally high level of bumbling incompetence in both establishments. I am not a vegetarian, and while I believe that food without meat can be delicious, I do not believe that real restaurants can be run on ideology. A restaurant is, after all, a business. Real restaurants work because the food is good, because the atmosphere is good, because customers feel comfortable in them. To be able to achieve these aims, the owners must love their restaurant. Most of the people working in these vegetarian restaurants did not love the restaurant; they loved not eating meat. It was, however, in these two establishments that I received my catering education and in some ways it was not too bad an education. I got used to the purchasing and preparing of food in quantity. I learned about ordering and stock-keeping and about the day-to-day running of a restaurant. When I left the second place, it was to attempt to open, with a partner, a restaurant of my own. This attempt almost succeeded, indeed would have done so, had it not been for a critical shortage of money. It was after this that I retired from catering and went into translating.

I wonder how often a course of action can be traced back to its origin? From the moment our friends suggested that it would be possible to turn our house into a restaurant, I began to consider the question again. In fact, if the truth be told, I became quite obsessed with the idea of restaurants, and didn't spare much thought to whether or not our combined qualifications were a reasonable basis for attempting to run one. I suppose I should also have considered whether our characters were of the right type for the catering trade. On the one hand, Sue is more than a little impatient, and likes to do everything very quickly, whereas a great deal of restaurant work is rather laborious and timeconsuming. She also requires the stimulus of new things happening all the time, but again, running a restaurant is a repetitive sort of job, where the same tasks have to be performed every day, especially washing up. Equally, waiting for customers to arrive every evening, given that they may arrive late, or may not turn up at all, is a terrible thing for someone who finds patience difficult. I, on the other hand, have a fairly easy-going attitude to life, and an optimistic tendency to improvise, or rely on my ability to get by at the last minute. In restaurant terms this might take the form of not preparing the elements of a *persillade* (a simple sauce of chopped parsley, minced garlic and melted butter) until someone actually orders one, on the grounds that I was not expecting one to be ordered. Fundamentally, this is laziness, and laziness is not at all a good quality for a restaurateur. On a more practical level, neither of us was good at working economically. In a domestic kitchen, it doesn't much matter if a little bit is wasted here and there: milk, butter, oil or flour. In a professional kitchen, waste of that sort – ten grams of sugar, half a cup of milk, a couple of tablespoonfuls of flour every day – can add up to hundreds of pounds over a year. This was something we learned from experience. On the plus side, although we had little real experience in the trade, we were both creditable cooks – in Sue's case very good indeed – and we both enjoyed cooking. Sue's French was embryonic when we opened, so there was no question of her doing the service. Besides, she is too shy to want to talk to 'a lot of strangers', as she calls the customers. But I am very fond, perhaps even too fond, of talking to people, and in a rather un-British way, I'm quite able to strike up a conversation with somebody I've never met before.

It is also true to say that we were both ready for different careers, and that's not a bad starting-point for opening a new business. Sue had just finished her first year as a doctor after passing her degree, and was thoroughly disenchanted with the National Health Service. Restaurant hours are very long, but they are not twenty-four hours a day long, and at least they are our own hours. Nor are we often called on to get up in the middle of the night, unless we have a sudden panic that we have forgotten to turn off the gas, or the stereo, or to lock the door of the restaurant.

At all events, some days after the conversation recounted above, I found myself sitting in the office of M. Faure at the Lyon Chambre de Commerce. In France, the Chambre de Commerce is a body which helps to promote commerce of all sorts, especially small businesses. It provides details of the formalities to be observed when undertaking alterations to premises, it informs on who must be contacted, which office in the Town Hall visited first, what fees paid, what documents deposited. M. Faure was a remarkable man. His dynamism was such that to spend five minutes with him was exhausting. After half an hour, one had to be helped to the door of his office. So powerful was his personality that as I reeled down the stairs and out into the street, the sky spinning above my head, I felt as though I was already the owner of a restaurant, and the very tired owner of a restaurant, at that.

M. Faure's first suggestion had been that I should buy an official Chambre de Commerce guide to restaurants, entitled *Créer et gérer son restaurant* ('Creating and running your restaurant'). I obtained a copy in Paris some days later. It is a slim paperback and I remember thinking that it was already an investment of considerable weight, since it cost 140 francs (about £16).

On the front cover is a cartoon by the French humorist, Amet. This represents a cook, in a chef's toque, with three pairs of hands, seemingly not attached to his body, suggesting that they are moving so fast that his arms cannot be seen. Beads of perspiration fly from his brow; he grins inanely. In one hand he holds a book entitled 'Basic Costs'. The five other hands variously crack eggs into a bowl, add seasoning, stir, taste and gesticulate frantically to some (probably imaginary) *aide-cuisine*. On either side of the bowl in front of him are further works with such titles as 'Law', 'Accounting', 'Management', 'Marketing', 'Finance', 'Stock-control'. This cover so disturbed me that I was never quite equal to opening *Créer et gérer* and to this day its contents remain dark to me.

What M. Faure informed us about planning permission for conversion of a commercial premises into a restaurant in France, was that the only people who could object were those living directly above the shop, and since we were those people we were scarcely likely to block our own planning application. Other rules to be respected were issued by the Safety and Hygiene Office and dealt with fire regulations, adequate evacuation of air from the kitchen, sufficient toilet facilities and so on. My next port of call was necessarily the bank.

2

My first visit to the bank was undertaken as a kind of recce, but in the event it was unnecessary to try another establishment. Our friend Alain Ville had secured a loan to purchase a car by maintaining that he was going to install some very expensive fitted kitchen equipment, since the interest rate was lower for home improvements than for car buying. The bank that had carried out this transaction was the Banque de Lyon et de sa Région, and while we had minds utterly free from all subterfuge, it did seem that a bank which could finance the installation of a fitted kitchen costing £9000 into a rented flat was perhaps the sort of institution which would advance money for creating an English restaurant in Lyon. It is, besides, a bank which concentrates on financing small businesses.

Our first contact was encouraging. The manager, Jean Dufour, gave an impression of utter reasonableness. He did not, for example, collapse into fits of uncontrollable laughter when I announced that I was going to set up an English restaurant around the corner from his bank. He said that his bank would look favourably on an application for a loan for such an undertaking, though of course could not be expected to finance it alone; various guarantees would be sought. We would have to put up a proportion of the cash. We would also have to submit a 'dossier'. What, I asked, would this dossier be expected to contain? The essential ingredients were as follows: a short introduction, or presentation of the project; an accountant's analysis, based on our figures and covering a three-year period; an analysis of the competition; a small market survey, obtained through a questionnaire; legal documents such as planning permission and my registration as a *commerçant* from the Lyon Régiste de Commerce; and quotations from all the artisans who were to carry out the alterations. Had I, by any chance, he continued, got a copy of the useful guide *Créer et gérer son restaurant* which gave information on the composition of a bank dossier? I said I kept it by my bed.

As it happened, the bank was persuaded to lend us the sum of money we needed without any guaranteeing collateral in the form of stocks and shares, real estate, art treasures and suchlike. This was a good thing, as we had none. At one stage, my father bravely offered the deeds of his house in the south of England as surety for the loan, but as the sum borrowed was only 175000 francs (around £20,000) the bank felt able to decline this offer. It is nonetheless true that French banks are notoriously unwilling to lend money on a speculative basis, unless the loan is guaranteed by property of equal value.

The item from the dossier which worried me the most was the market survey by street questionnaire. The reason for this was that I could not help feeling that the average Frenchman, stopped in the street and asked to give his opinion on the opening of an English restaurant in Lyon, would be inclined to bridle with chauvinism at any idea of a culinary assault on his nation's status as World Cooking Rulers. I was concerned that a French person in these circumstances would feel a strong inclination to say *'n'importe quoi'*, or shoot his mouth off, as we might say in English.

I drafted the questionnaire with the help of a friend who had some experience in market research. The thing to do, apparently, was to allow the questionee as little opportunity as possible for self expression. Questions should only permit the answers 'yes' or 'no', or at the most a number: how many times a month do you dine out? The drafting went fairly rapidly, until we came to the last two questions. Our final version read as follows: 'An English restaurant is to be established in Lyon. Do you find this idea (a) interesting or (b) grotesque?' The following question was quite simply 'Why?' This was the one question in which we were asking the public to think a little. We were uncertain as to the exact terms in which to phrase the question, and decided to go out into the street to test it on the first passers-by we came across. These turned out to be two students, aged about twenty. 'An English restaurant is to be established in Lyon', we intoned. 'Do you find this idea (a) interesting or (b) grotesque?'

'Grotesque!' flashed back the young man instantly.

'Why?'

'Because of the policies of Margaret Thatcher.'

I immediately realized that there was absolutely no point whatsoever in pursuing this market research idea, and that a far more realistic picture would be obtained by my inventing the results of the survey and presenting them clearly in percentage form: 63 per cent of those interviewed said that they would appreciate a selection of whiskies offered at prices not exceeding . . .

I mentioned above that no subterfuge was employed in obtaining the loan from the bank, but it has to be admitted that a certain amount of deviousness seemed difficult to avoid, was, indeed, even encouraged. At one point M. Dufour informed me that it would be easier to obtain the loan if I had had five years of catering experience. Had I no way, he asked, looking me in the eye, of showing that although I had only two years' experience (and these two already grossly exaggerated), had I no way of showing that I had in fact five? The hint was duly taken, and my next move was to have headed notepaper printed for myself in the name of a London restaurant owned by my brotherin-law some years before. I then wrote a reference for myself, saying that I had completed five years of loyal service for this restaurant, had fulfilled many different roles adequately, and had always kept my hand out of the till. To give the thing an air of verisimilitude. I had my brother-in-law sign it. On a scale of dishonesty ranging from one to ten, I felt that these acts scored very lowly.

For our analysis of the competition, we simply visited all the other restaurants in the area and then awarded them points out of ten for décor, service, friendliness, quality of food and so forth. More tricky was our registration as *commerçants* at the Lyon Régiste de Commerce, for this involved the storming of the bastions of French bureaucracy, where the French warrior-bureaucrats are even more firmly entrenched behind their desks than their English counterparts. Armed to the hilt with lethal documents, they refuse to give intelligible answers to telephone enquiries as to which papers must be brought to them for their inspection.

'You must bring', they state, '*un maximum de documentation.*' And yet, no matter how complete the maximum in question, there always seems to be something missing. However, as a point of information, if ever you should think of undertaking a similar move to France to establish a business, then a sensible minimum of documents is as follows: passport, full birth certificates of your entire family and also, if you have one, your marriage certificate. These papers must be translated into French by a translator accredited by the French administration. When converting your driving licence to a French one, you will also need to have that translated by an accredited translator. It is no use doing it yourself, even if you have been, as I was, an international translator; the French version must be stamped (and paid for). You will also need the deeds of your property, or a copy of the lease in your name, together with some absolute proof that you live in the place you claim, something solid, like a recent gas, electricity or phone bill, addressed to you at the address indicated on the lease. In France, gas and electricity bills play a significant role in proof of identity and residence.

Theoretically, there is no objection to anyone coming from within the EC establishing a business in any one of the EC countries. M. Faure had explained to me where I had to go and in which order. However, there was no knowing how closely the French civil servants would resemble M. Faure's image of simple, smiling people, cheerily stamping on various forms 'pass', 'move directly to go', 'collect £200 if you pass go', that sort of thing. The reality was very often quite different from this. Of course, it is clear that any administration has to keep track of what is going on, otherwise, especially in a country with inhabitants as wilful and anarchic as the French, chaos would manifestly reign. The trouble is that the officers of the French administration seem so often to take exquisite pleasure in impeding forward motion, and delight in sending you scuttling sideways, crabwise. An example of this was my attempt to obtain a *carte membre de la CEE* (EEC membership card).

This card was of prime necessity for my registration at the Régiste de Commerce. It was the first document I had to obtain. I rang the *préfecture* (the town hall) to ask them what documents they would require to issue me with such an item.

'We cannot answer inquiries by telephone. You must make an appointment and bring a maximum of documentation'. I duly made an appointment and arrived at the hour indicated. Administrative offices are always depressing places and this one was no exception. Since it was the immigration office, it was filled with families from Morocco, Tunisia, Algeria, the Ivory Coast, Senegal and so on, and I had the impression that they had been bivouacking there for some months. Certainly, there was much evidence of meals being taken, babies changed and clothes repaired and altered. I was finally called to the desk. I explained that I was British and was about to open a restaurant in Lyon, and that I required the *carte membre de la CEE*.

'*Très bien*,' said the woman, 'we shall need to see your registration at the Régiste de Commerce.'

'It's interesting that you should ask me for that,' I said, 'because according to the officers of that organization, I cannot be registered there without first having my EEC card.' The administrative officer settled herself more securely behind her desk.

'I'm afraid it is impossible.'

'What must I do?'

'Return to the Régiste de Commerce.'

'But I was there three days ago, and they explained clearly that they needed the *carte membre de la CEE* before they could register me.'

'We cannot advance your documentation without your registration. It is an absolute necessity.'

Eventually, M. Faure put all to rights with a couple of phone calls. It is always as well to have a contact on the inside.

There is no doubt, however, that the art of prevarication

carried to such a pitch throughout an entire administration can drive people insane. On my first visit to the Régiste de Commerce the number of people sitting in the waiting room made me realize that the best way to attack that particular office would be to arrive in the morning at least half an hour before opening time. On this first occasion, I had vaguely noticed a machine on the top wall of the waiting room which issued numbered tickets. The following day I arrived at half-past eight in the morning, to find that I was the second person there. Some moments later we were joined by a third person, who began to chat to person number one in a slightly manic way.

By the time it was nine o'clock, there were about thirty people waiting at the door. From somewhere above us, a clock started to toll the hour. There were clangings and creaks as multiple locks were loosed on the other side of the door. The crowd pushed forward in anticipation.

'Now,' said arrivee number three, 'let's get this straight.' He pointed to number one. 'You were first,' he said; then to me, 'and you were second, and I', he indicated himself, 'I was third.'

'I think there's a system of tickets inside,' I said.

'Yes,' he said, 'but we must establish the order.' With that, the doors sprung open and we all surged forward into the long narrow room. I had time to notice that on the far wall there was a shelf with three stacks of forms on it, pink, yellow and green. Above them were two ticket machines, one distributing pink tickets and the other yellow tickets. An official announced in a loud voice that all those wishing to complete form 662B (or some such number) should take

a yellow ticket and a yellow form, while all those requiring a
331C should take a pink form and a pink ticket. Person
number one and I arrived in front of the shelf and looked
desperately at the pink, yellow and green forms. None of
them seemed to apply. I took a green form and seized a pink
ticket. In the meantime, number one had taken a pink form
and a yellow ticket. Number three pounced like a cat.

'Aha,' he said, 'I see that you have a green form and a pink
ticket, and you have a pink form and a yellow ticket: *ça ne
va pas*. I'm going in first.' And before we knew what was
happening he had slipped past us and was sitting in front of
a desk with what were, no doubt, the correct papers for his
particular transaction. Number one and I were completely
flabbergasted. In our confusion, several other people passed
in front of us as well.

Eventually all the administrative details were accom-
plished and my dossier was complete. I had come to realize
two things about presenting a dossier to a French bank –
possibly to any bank in the world. The first was that the
compilation of such a document is really a series of tests, a
kind of trial by fire to see whether the applicant has the force
of character to win through. 'Look,' I imagined the bank
saying, 'he has even managed to obtain a *carte membre de la
CEE*. It is clear that Mr Higgins is *un type bien, sérieux*.'
The bank manager was transformed in my imagination into
a kind of bewimpled medieval maiden: 'Go, fetch me a form
662B and bring it hither, for verily I say to you, never my
love shall be yours until you have done this thing for me.'
And off into the darkest corridors of the French Administration rides the knight errant. The second thing was that the

appearance of the dossier was all-important. I made a terrific effort with mine. Much time was spent in office supply shops seeking precisely the right kind of file in which to keep the papers: something that looked clean and modern, and also presented the information in such a way that it was easy to look at (and believe). Maps to show where we were, photographs of the outside of the house, artist's impressions, the architect's plans: a place was found for all these things. In the end, it was so beautiful that I didn't want to give it to the bank at all; I just wanted to keep it for myself and look at it.

Such feelings were simply the result of mounting hysteria. The bank duly received its copy of the dossier and, true to his word, Jean Dufour produced the cash. My first visit to the bank had been in early June 1985. The dossier was handed over towards the end of September, and in November we were ready to begin work. We had spent the intervening months exploring the city and the countryside around it, and, I have to admit, indulging in a certain amount of delaying tactics on my part, since work, when it did begin, began with an act of destruction: the demolition of the ground floor of our house.

3

We first came through Lyon about eight years ago. It was at lunchtime on a Sunday in August, and the town was utterly deserted. It must have been ninety in the shade. The streets were empty, dusty and white with heat. The air was bent by the power of the sun. Imaginary pools of water appeared in the road in front of the car and buildings a few hundred yards distant seemed to be shaky mirages. For me, it was love at first sight. Imagine a city which is big enough to be interesting – big enough to contain innumerable cinemas, theatres, galleries – but not so big that you can't walk around it, or at least, walk from one side of the city centre to the other. Imagine a city that is perfectly placed in beautiful countryside which you can get to in less than half an hour. There simply aren't many places like Lyon. Paris and Geneva are two hours' train ride away. The best skiing in Europe is an hour and a half away by car. The lunar landscape of Le Puy lies just to the west, the Bugey and the Jura are to the east, Valence and the Midi to the south, and to the north, the rolling hills of the Beaujolais and Burgundy regions.

This – the ease with which you can leave it – is one of the most marvellous things about Lyon, an advantage which it holds over larger cities like Paris and London. Paris is a vast, sprawling expanse, almost impossible to escape from at weekends, let alone for a few hours during the week. If you do succeed in getting out, the two directions in which you are almost certain to go are towards Rouen or to Deauville. Returning on the Sunday evening, unless you aim to arrive either very early or very late, you will be greeted by an entirely stationary block of traffic around the *boulevard périphérique*. Moreover, the areas around Rouen and Deauville are so flooded with Parisians at weekends and bank holidays that they are transformed into extensions of the Faubourg Saint-Germain.

We have a picnic spot in the Beaujolais which we can reach within forty minutes of leaving our house. Under no circumstances will I reveal its precise whereabouts, but, set as it is in a large cherry orchard amongst the vineyards round the village of Lachassagne, it is fairly typical of Beaujolais scenery. For all I know, this spot may be a favourite place for Lyonnais picnics on Saturday and Sunday, but we work on those days, and are free to go to the place on Mondays, when there is no one else around. Once, lying in the shade under the fruit trees on a hot summer afternoon we saw a couple of deer break from the cover of thick undergrowth and race across the field in front of us, to plunge back into the forest on the other side of the field. The deer were pale gold, and the earth, dried by the sun, was the same colour. The scene seemed curiously medieval.

The Beaujolais could almost be called a mountainous area, with peaks rising to nearly 1000 metres. The land is intensely cultivated, covered either with beautifully planted rows of vines, their roots packed around with rocks, or with cherry, plum, apple or greengage orchards. Tomatoes, strawberries and raspberries are also grown. These areas of dense cultivation are broken up by the wooded peaks of hills too high to be made over to farming, or by patches of oak and beech forest, full of giant trees. I am very fond of the Beaujolais, and find it hard to restrain the lyrical mood it inspires in me, but the best thing about it is that it is so close to Lyon, and offers such a contrast with city life.

The River Saône flows through Burgundy and the Beaujolais, irrigating some of the most famous vineyards in the world. Lyon lies at the confluence of the Rhône and the Saône. The centre of the town which has become the main shopping area, is squeezed on to the spit of land, or peninsula, between these two rivers. The Rhône comes twisting through the mountains to the east, its waters green and full of melting ice. The passage it cuts through the mountains via Bellegarde is often spectacular, and the journey eastwards to Geneva is a very beautiful one. By the time the river reaches Lyon, it must be almost 200 metres across.

Lyon is well known to most tourists, French tourists included, as the town where there are hellish traffic jams at holiday periods. The motorway from Paris down to the south of France passes directly through the city. A bypass is being built, but bypass or no bypass, if tourists hit the Rhône corridor at the wrong time, they'll be condemned to swelter in traffic jams around Lyon. And worse, if they miss the bypass, they'll get stuck in one of the tunnels through which the motorway passes. The number of people I have met who have said that they know Lyon, then qualify the statement by saying 'Well, I've passed through it', is astonishing. Generally, this remark is followed by a faint expression of intense torment which flashes across their faces, and I know that they are remembering the tunnels. How, they are thinking, can anyone live in a place like that?

And yet, Lyon is a beautiful city. I believe it would be difficult to find a more agreeable city in Europe. It deserves a proper visit, and it deserves someone to sing its praises a bit. A city with one river is already interesting; a city with two, doubly so. Each river has its share of fine bridges, with beautiful houses on their banks. But Lyon is a town which keeps itself to itself, which is perhaps not even fully aware of what it possesses. The scale of its architecture is not at the palatial level of Paris. It is a city not for giants, but for humans, and the pleasure is not overawing, but domestic. It's a city to live in.

The oldest parts of the town are on the right-hand bank of the Saône. The Romans built an aqueduct into the city from the west, and large portions of it remain. In the areas of Saint-Just and Fourvière, 17th- and 18th-century builders squeezed rows of houses in between the piers of this aqueduct. Possibly the construction was too solid, too massive to demolish, so it simply had to be incorporated. Further in towards the centre of town are two amphitheatres, used nowadays for concerts, plays and operas. I suppose that neither of these could be described as beautiful, but they are still impressive structures: buildings from 2000 years ago hedged in on all sides by modern blocks. Along the right bank of the Saône is the medieval quarter of Saint-Jean. A lot of this area has been renovated, and it contains a warren of narrow cobbled streets, lined with beautiful early Renaissance buildings. The cathedral of Saint-Jean, which gives the area its name, has a rather cold, unimaginative Gothic façade, and inside a bewildering automated clock dating from the 16th century. Every hour, about a dozen small jointed figures are set into jerky motion, finally stilled by a Swiss soldier who tolls the hour on a bell at the summit of the clock. Even so long ago, presumably centuries before the invention of the first cuckoo clock, it seems that the Swiss had a reputation for keeping the time.

Saint-Jean is an area where there are many nightclubs, bars, discotheques and restaurants. But it is not an area where you will necessarily eat either very well or very cheaply. The volume of passing tourist trade is sufficient to fill most of the restaurants regularly, without their having to make much effort. On the other hand, the terms 'expensive' and 'not very good', have to be taken in context; the general Lyonnais standard is higher, and the general price lower than in restaurants elsewhere. What I find interesting about Saint-Jean is that, despite the tourist-oriented trade, the area has an authentic, lived-in feeling about it. There are still old *boulangeries*, *épiceries* and *fromageries*. Down one of the darker alleyways, push open a door here or there: it may reveal a perfect cantilevered stone staircase, a courtyard with a fountain, a vaulted chamber or a *traboule* – a passageway leading through the houses and out into the road on the other side of the block of buildings. In another city, a great deal of fuss would be made about these details, and perhaps Lyon will begin to fuss about them soon, but for the moment my impression is that they are pretty much taken for granted.

Passing across one of the many bridges from Saint-Jean into the centre of town takes you onto the spit of land separating the two rivers before they join a few kilometres downstream. This part of town is called the Presqu'île. On the left bank of the Saône, facing you as you cross the bridge, are rows of elegant 18th- and 19th-century buildings, all painted in beautiful shades of cream, pink and beige. Overlooking the town at the top of a steep hill above Saint-Jean is an extraordinary basilica built in the late 19th century. It's a rectangular building with four hefty, round towers, one at each corner. The Lyonnais refer to it deprecatingly as *l'éléphant*, since it resembles one of those beasts lying on its back with its legs in the air. Just to the right of this church is what looks like Eiffel's first attempt at a tower – a miniature version of the famous Parisian monument, in fact the work of another engineer altogether.

Most of the buildings on the Presqu'île date from the 18th and 19th centuries. The area contains the Musée des Beaux Arts, the town hall, one of the mainline stations, the Place Bellecour – one of the biggest squares in Europe – a number of medieval churches and a magnificent 17th-century hospi-

tal, the Hôtel Dieu. Of course, there is far too much traffic in
the centre of town, but some of the streets have been pedestrianized, the buildings are fine and the shops good, and a
stroll through the city streets remains a real pleasure. Many
of the restaurants are concentrated in a remarkable Renaissance street, the Rue Mércière. Here again, prices are high
and quality somewhat lacking, but then the restaurants
have wide terraces, the street is so pretty and there are so
many people, that it is worth going to eat there just for the
show. At night in the summer you can sit out on one of
the terraces of the pedestrianized Rue de la République, and
watch a continuous stream of jugglers, sword-swallowers,
buskers, acrobats, fire-eaters, mimes and clowns go past.
Naturally, they all hand round a hat after each performance
and after about an hour it becomes boring to be constantly
importuned. Then it is time to move on somewhere quieter.

Across the Presqu'île you arrive at the Rhône. On the far
side the buildings are late 19th- and early 20th-century:
quite grand, but not of particular architectural merit. There
is an outstandingly beautiful park, supposedly laid out in
the English style, called Parc de la Tête d'Or. It contains a
lovely botanic garden and many fascinating greenhouses,
some of which are very tall, Crystal Palace-like structures.
There is even a creditable zoo. It must be said that some of
the animals are kept in distressing conditions – notably the
bears, whose cage is a very dismal affair indeed – but this is
soon to be remedied. An utterly charming turn-of-the-
century carousel, with its original pipe-organ, attracts many
children.

Next to the park lies the most exclusive area of Lyon: the

sixth *arrondissement*. This is an expensive residential area containing few bars and restaurants, but many expensive shops; the district is admittedly '*très bon pour le shopping*'. The Lyonnais who do not live in the *sixième* have a tendency to make disparaging remarks about the inhabitants of that area. They are supposed to be particularly snobbish, to look down on all other areas of town, and in general, to have far too much money for their own good. This would not be so bad, if they were not also notable for their lack of imagination and taste, which makes it impossible for them to spend it in a reasonable way. In fact, to say that someone is '*très sixième*' is not very polite. As a foreigner, I do my best to remain aloof from this kind of petty squabbling, but I feel bound to remark on a recent fashion among little girls aged between four and eight, which was exclusive to the *sixième* and to my knowledge did not spread outside it. For some reason the *petites élégantes* of that area took it into their heads to flap around in mid-calf-length skirts, garments which, it must be admitted, are not absolutely practical for active youngsters. The decision of these little girls to go around like miniature versions of their Edwardian great-grandmothers could be, and certainly was, described as '*très sixième*'. Needless to say, a great many of the people who castigate this area and its inhabitants also aspire one day to live in it.

Further east lies the terrible area of the Part Dieu. Here, all the old buildings are being demolished and replaced with the sort of modern structures which look so impressive as architects' models, but considerably less so when they are built. On a tiny scale, with miniature cars (not too many) and lots of trees and gardens, the aerial walkways, moving staircases and even the multi-storey car-parks look jolly fine. The reality is a depressing mess of concrete blocks already looking shabby, divided by the sort of urban racetracks so dear to the hearts of certain French motorists. Construction techniques have been employed which appear to have succumbed almost immediately to the test of time. The area is built around Lyon's main station, La Part Dieu, and the biggest indoor shopping centre in Europe – or is it the world? At any rate, the Part Dieu commercial centre, although it contains many wonderful shops, and even the Lyon branch of Marks & Spencer, is, for me, an awful place.

The area in which we live is called the Croix-Rousse. It is the fourth *arrondissement* of Lyon. It is situated above the Presqu'île, on a hill overlooking the rest of the town. This hill is very steep and very densely populated, the buildings stacked up the slope in high banks, row upon row, climbing up the hill. Since all, or many, of these houses are painted in a range of pastel colours, the Croix-Rousse is an impressive, picturesque sight when viewed from below, recalling Cézanne's many views of the Mont Sainte-Victoire in Provence. Equally, on the summit of the hill, from certain places where there is a break in the buildings, an esplanade or a garden, there are wonderful views over the town below, and beyond, across the Rhône valley, it is sometimes possible to see the white mass of the Alps rising in the distance. It is an area which grew up in the 18th and 19th centuries, gradually spreading up the hill (Croix-Rousse Pentes) and over the top (Croix-Rousse Plateau) with the great expansion in Lyon's silk production. Almost all the buildings of the Croix-Rousse are former silk workshops, and the result is near-total homogeneity of architecture. The buildings are handsome, in the same way that an 18th-century cloth-mill in Britain is handsome. They can be up to six storeys high – even higher on the slopes of the hill – and are normally four or six bays across. The ceilings are very lofty, sometimes 15 or 16 feet, since the machines used to produce silk were large. It is consequently possible, when transforming the old *ateliers* into apartments, to install a mezzanine floor. Sometimes you cannot stand upright on these floors, but they provide additional sleeping room or office space. This idea is not a new one: in the old days, silk workers would sleep on such mezzanines, then descend to work in the area below during the day.

Nowadays there is very little silk production left in Lyon since the old techniques have been replaced by more modern methods, and silk is largely imported from the Far East. It is also true that the heavy, brocaded silk for which Lyon was famous went out of fashion in the early years of this century. The few workshops left produce material for the restoration of hangings and furnishings in the palaces of Europe. They are probably down to their last ten years of production, before the techniques die out altogether.

The Croix-Rousse has become, I suppose, the rough equivalent of the Montmartre area of Paris – the artists' quarter. There is, however, more emphasis on artisan trade than on artistic production. There are many furniture makers, plumbers, leather workers, antique restorers, wrought iron *ateliers*. Fashion jewellery is made here, and diamond setting is another activity. *Boulangeries, char-*

cutiers, traiteurs, fromageries, pâtisseries, butchers and all suppliers of food abound. There are a multitude of old-fashioned bars, one very respectable hotel and another which seems far from respectable, and a fair number of restaurants. There are many excellent shops, parks, gardens, a wide, leafy boulevard. It is, in fact, an absolutely enchanting area; a self-contained village within ten minutes' walk of the city centre, whose inhabitants claim to be Croix-Roussien rather than Lyonnais. It is never really necessary to go down into the centre of town in the normal course of events, but the number 6 bus ride, which takes you down, is the nicest in Lyon, winding through the vertiginous streets of the Croix-Rousse Pentes, then suddenly emerging on to a parapet overlooking another, third, amphitheatre and affording a marvellous view across the rooftops of the town to the medieval quarter beyond. The area is undergoing that curious phenomenon of 'coming up' and up it inevitably will come, since it has so many advantages. Not least of these, for a restaurateur, is a street market held every day except Monday, which vies with the market on the Quai Saint-Antoine in the town centre as the best in Lyon.

Our house is in a street set back from the main square of the Croix-Rousse. From a driver's point of view the street is something of an enigma, since it has no entry signs at both its ends, and must be approached from a road which cuts it in half. It cannot be said that the restaurant is especially well situated. We have now been here for eight years, and it is still possible to meet people who live around the corner and have not heard of our existence. The house had previously been a *boulangerie,* though bread production had ceased ten years before. In fact, the last baker sold his ovens and his concession to the other bakers in the area, who bought them simply to reduce the competition. The previous tenant, our friend Alain Ville, had carried out a good deal of conversion work on what must have been a fairly unprepossessing structure. The house, which was built at the end of the 18th century and originally intended as silk *ateliers*, has a four-bay façade a little over thirty feet across, with a depth of twenty feet at its deepest point. The ground floor was a lock-up shop, and Alain had left the façade as it was: a 1970s aluminium shop window, which he had rendered opaque with curtains, lace and otherwise. The front door was a glass shop door that he had had sand-blasted. There are two floors and an attic above the ground floor, reached by a common staircase. Below is a marvellous vaulted cellar, which mysteriously maintains its temperature all the year round, irrespective of summers when the temperature rises to 45 degrees centigrade, and winters where it falls to minus 15. What Alain decided to do was to turn the ground floor into his kitchen and bathroom, then connect it, with an internal staircase, to the first floor flat, which became his bedroom and sitting-room. Now, the principal glory of these houses is their ceilings, *plafonds à la française*. Great solid oak beams, known as *poutres*, run from the front to the back of the house, joined transversely by a framework of smaller beams, or *chevrons*. Sand-blasted – as they invariably are by the *jeunes cadres dynamiques* (yuppies) who are gradually moving into the area – to remove all traces of paint or dirt, they are revealed to be a beautiful golden brown. (Personally, I prefer all my ceilings painted: they were made to be filled and painted, and if they are sand-blasted, then dust and pebbles are constantly falling out of them.) But the real beauty of these ceilings from our point of view was their construction: only the main beams are load-bearing, and they carry the weight of the whole house, so that if you wished it, each floor could be one enormous room. Our house was just asking to be converted to a restaurant.

4

Demolition began one day early in November. I had enlisted the help of an extremely small, though very tough, friend called Jean Lextrait, whom I had met years before in London. Jean is the best possible painter and decorator imaginable, achieving standards of finish far beyond the expectations of his employers. In a way, this has been his downfall. When giving quotations for jobs, he has failed to take into account his own perfectionism, and the result has been far too much time spent on jobs for a fixed, pre-agreed price. On that morning in November, we breakfasted together for a last time in the kitchen downstairs, then, armed with crowbars, saws, drills and sledgehammers, we smashed the place to pieces. Jean handed me the sledgehammer, suggesting that I might like to take the first swing. I gave the wall nearest to me a rather gingerly tap, producing a faint dent in the surface. 'Not like that,' he said, taking the hammer and raising it up to shoulder height, 'like this.' And the hammer crashed through layers of brick and plasterboard and cement.

For me, the demolition of the ground floor of the house is inextricably linked with the Story of the Rat, although this epic tale dates back to some time before the demolition began. We had left the house empty for over a month while away on holiday, and were much distressed on our return to find that we had mice. At least, we thought they were mice at first. We continued to refer to them as mice, despite the fact that the noises they made were out of all proportion to their supposed size, and long after we had realized, in our heart of hearts, that here we were concerned with creatures of a larger variety.

The houses in this area, as I have said, are old. Their cellars may be even older, the foundations of earlier dwellings. Who knows what myriad galleries, what labyrinthine subterranean passages the mice and rats of this and earlier centuries may not have constructed for themselves? Occasional rodent invasions, especially in view of the quantity of food-selling establishments in the area, are only to be expected. Our first step in dealing with ours was to use poison. Little trays of bright blue corn were left in strategic areas, with a concentration under the sink, which appeared to be Rodent Headquarters. How they loved that stuff! They simply couldn't get enough of it. On one occasion there was a bowl of it under the sink, as well as a packet on the shelf just above. Ratty, for we now realized that it was he, having finished the bowl, tried to make off with the bag and its contents. Unfortunately, it would not fit into his hole.

Ratty became obsessed with the dustbin. It was unquestionably his favourite place and he left it only with the greatest reluctance on the approach of man. The trouble was, and I believe that Ratty started to understand this, his reluctance to leave the dustbin on the approach of man was no greater than man's own reluctance to approach the Ratty-containing dustbin. He was beginning to lose that fear proper to small animals of those creatures much bigger than themselves, and we realized that it was time to do something drastic. The man in the shop informed us that if poison was not working, then a trap was the only way. A trap was purchased. I was tired of coming downstairs making as much noise as I could, to frighten the rat away and thus avoid a man-to-rat combat. The trap was put into position, baited and set.

It seems to me that I lay awake that night, waiting to hear the snap of the trap as it sprang. I believe that I did hear that trap, echoing through my fitful dreams, tearing the shreds of an uncertain sleep, yet a descent in the middle of the night was unthinkable. Early the next morning I slowly went down the stairs. Either result was bound to be distressing: not catching the beast would mean intensified hunting; catching him, an undertaking job and the end of a relationship that had lasted over two weeks. As it happened, Ratty was dead. It felt like the end of an era.

Some days later, Jean and I were approaching the end of the demolition. One small section of wall had been left behind the sink, which the plumber came in to disconnect on a Monday morning. I had been working alone in the shop over Saturday and Sunday and it had seemed to me that I had detected faint rustlings from behind this last remaining piece of wall left standing, though knowing that Ratty was no more made me dismiss these as the product of my imagination. It was Jean who achieved this last piece of demolition, while I busied myself, probably unnecessarily, outside. When I re-entered the shop, an extraordinary sight greeted my eyes. Jean was leaping between piles of rubble, flailing out wildly with a crowbar. Then I saw it: Ratty II. Now, at this point, I am ashamed to say that my courage failed and I beat a very hasty retreat into the street. But this lapse was only momentary. Within a second I was back inside the shop, to block off Ratty's exit. Stories I had heard of cornered rats jumping at their aggressors' faces and scratching their eyes were all but banished from my mind. Luckily for Ratty, and for me, his exit was nowhere near where I was standing, and he disappeared through a hole in the wall, never to be seen or heard of again.

The demolition continued; we filled two skips with the rubble. The street was fascinated by what was going on, and dozens of people stopped to ask what was going to be installed. '*Un restaurant anglais?*' they said; '*C'est pas possible!*' Others asked us if the premises were really big enough for a restaurant. Well, on the plans it all fitted in, but I did begin to have my doubts. I had visions of the stove and fridge arriving and there being no place to put them. In the local bistro opposite us, the Café du Commerce, bets were being placed as to how long we would last if we ever opened. On our side of the street, we demolished the façade and felt more exposed than ever. The ground floor resembled a cave: rough, unfaced stone walls, no light, the floor all broken to pieces. The façade was three gaping holes, like a row of doorless garages. We blocked these off with our version of the obligatory palisade, an altogether minimalist structure. It was time for the experts to move in and begin the business of rebuilding.

An interior designer was engaged to draw up plans and coordinate the operation of reconstruction. Jean-Pierre Biancamaria was a friend already before the restaurant, and has remained so since. This is a major testament to his ability, when you consider that his job consists largely of spending considerable quantities of someone else's money, and then receiving payment for doing so. Of course, the project is carefully planned first: quotations are drawn up, compared, rejected and so forth, and a budget is set out, based on the amount which can be repaid each month.

I am more or less certain that old-fashioned restaurants – or at least restaurants that look old-fashioned – appeal to customers more easily than modern ones. People, when they go out for a meal, like to take a step back into the past, with all its genuine feel: solid wood seats and tables, old tiled floors, gleaming glassware on polished shelves in front of cut-glass mirrors; dark, reassuring interiors, the odd light-bulb not working, the ceiling perhaps a little yellow from generations of smokers; memories of pure food, before the days of pre-packed, vacuum-preserved products, deep-freezes and additives; even the golden summers of yesteryear may be evoked. I have known restaurants work on the basis of their appearance alone; providing the food is neither too awful, nor too expensive, it may still be highly prefabricated, but the public – at least the vast, not very discriminating majority of it – is taken in by the show.

Thus, up to a certain point, atmosphere in a restaurant is more important than the quality of the cooking. It is understandable that people should want to escape from their own world a little when they go out to eat, and they do not necessarily want to escape into the future – an unknown country if ever there was one. But to slip back into the past, that is a different matter. Innumerable bars in France are filled with young people who imagine themselves sitting there supping absinthe with Sartre and Cocteau, rubbing shoulders with Picasso and Braques, the Ballets Russes, the Revue Noire, Josephine Baker, all that. In our case, however, we had only our bare shell of a ground floor, with its three gaping holes. To create something that looked old-fashioned would have been very expensive, and false. Besides, Jean-Pierre only does contemporary interior design. While he is prepared to use old elements – such as an old bar, fireplace or mirror – he will not produce something that looks Art Nouveau or Art Deco. It will look modern. However, he is an extremely able interior designer, and his interiors are never cold, futuristic design sets where you feel uncomfortable if not dressed up to the nines in the very latest fashions.

The design was necessarily simple. The space is a rectangle, with a square cut out of one corner. The longer side lies along the façade of the building, facing out on to the street through the three window openings. The kitchen and the lavatories were to be located at the back, in the narrower part. Thus, the restaurant dining room is about 30 feet long by 15 feet deep. This gives enough space for ten tables, with a maximum of thirty seats. Jean-Pierre designed beautiful French windows to fill the gaping holes in the wall, and these are glazed in different sorts of glass – some coloured, some opaque and some clear. The wall between the kitchen and the restaurant is also glazed in the same way. Lighting is indirect, from half-moon wall lights, throwing the light up on to a white ceiling. There is a dimmer-switch, and with something in the way of 4000 watts of halogen light-bulb on tap, a pretty low regulation is selected. The restaurant does not really have intimate little corners, so dimmish lighting in the evening is more pleasant. The walls were painted by spray-gun in a sort of pinky-oatmeal colour, while all the window-frames have hammerite-finish blue paint on them. The chairs are chrome-plated, angular-looking things, but are so well designed that, although made out of bare metal, they are very comfortable.

Jean-Pierre, like all good interior designers, made us feel that we were responsible for the whole thing, when in fact he had come to us with ideas, samples, suggestions, and said 'You could have this, or this, but perhaps *this* is the best.' I chose the wall lights, but he told me where to go and look. I chose the chairs, but from a range Jean-Pierre had told me about. If I was absolutely responsible for any part of the design, then it was the floor. I said that I wanted a wooden parquet floor and that I wanted it stained green. Afterwards, parquets stained different colours became part of Jean-Pierre's design 'vocabulary', and began to be seen in shops and flats around Lyon. When we had it done, many people were shocked. We are, after all, in the land of the sand-blasted, natural wood ceiling.

The rebuilding of the blackened hole into a designerish interior took about two and a half months. It could have gone much more quickly, but I indulged in a good deal of dragging of heels. Much of the time I was away working in Geneva or elsewhere and I can remember ringing poor Sue, who had to put up with living in a building site, and asking whether they had fitted the doors, whether the ceiling was in place, whether the basin had been put into the bathroom. The first workmen to appear were the electricians and plumbers. Both were artisans who had been selected because they had workshops in our street and because of their air of old-world dependability. M. Reymond the electrician hung festoons of wire about the walls and ceiling and spoke to me darkly of things referred to as *monophasé* and *triphasé*. I hadn't the faintest notion what these things represented, though on his advice I opted for the latter. It appeared that more power would be available to us if we used *triphasé*, and that the French electricity board was jealous of its amperes (after all, a French discovery), and only allotted them begrudgingly – despite being, I believe, Europe's biggest producer of electricity. As Jean-Pierre was rapidly multiplying the amount of halogen light bulbs, electrical heating and air-conditioning, power, it seemed, was what we needed.

M. Farge, the plumber, was a phlegmatic character. His name always sounded to me like the name of an ancient but indispensable plumbing tool – 'Pass me the farge, will you, I just have to tighten the seal on this grommet' – or a highly specialized plumbing technique: 'I've had the water tank re-farged, and the difference has been amazing.' One after-noon while he was working away, I came down from the flat upstairs with the offer of a cup of tea. '*Ah non*,' said Farge in reply to my proposal, '*ça, jamais*.' I think that if I'd sug-gested a trip across the road to the Commerce for a *coup de rouge* he might have snapped it up. I was always worried to look across at the Café du Commerce in the morning at about half-past seven and to see Farge in there with his workman Pietri, drinking a carafe of white wine. The older type of French workman considers white wine to be a stimulant, much like coffee – indeed, a reasonable sub-situtute for that drink. Because of this, they will rarely drink it at night, for fear of not sleeping. Pietri and Farge would then arrive and set to work. Two hours later, around ten o'clock, they were again to be seen across the road, pa-tronizing the Commerce with another jug of white wine. Work stopped at twelve, which was time to go back to the Commerce for several aperitifs. Lunch, also taken at the Commerce, would involve a certain amount of red wine. The afternoon would be divided by visits to the Commerce to consume more wine or possibly a glass or two of beer, and the day would end with a pre-dinner aperitif (also at the Commerce), before heading off home. It was presumably during these visits that the bets concerning our business venture were placed.

Once the electrical and plumbing work had been finished, the window frames and the kitchen walls were installed. The former were designed by Jean-Pierre and made up out of square-section steel tubing by Marcel Gay, the locksmith.

I am not sure how easy it would be to have such a thing made to measure in Britain, since they are an extraordinarily impressive piece of work – not only because they are so complicated, but because in an old building like this, not one of the front openings can be identical in size to another, and yet the façade gives an impression of perfect symmetry. They cost about £700 each, and for complex pieces of precisely forged metal-work, measuring over 8 feet high and about 5 feet across, that cannot be thought of as expensive.

Salvatore Falsone, a second-generation Italian immigrant to France, relined our walls with plasterboard. The French love to build in *placopâtres* and *carreaux de plâtre*. The *placoplâtres* are sheets of plasterboard, the *carreaux de plâtre* are big interlocking squares of cast plaster which fit together like lego and can be used to build up interior partition walls. It is a pretty rubbishy sort of building material, but it is very quick, since each *carreau* measures 2 feet square. They are stuck together with plaster glue. One of their principal qualities is that they are utter bliss to knock down with a sledgehammer, since they shatter so satisfyingly. Salvatore Falsone was a nice man who looked like a stage Italian – rather red in the face, with thick, curly hair and a very black moustache. His hobby was trumpet playing, and it was very easy to imagine him tooting away on a bugle, getting even redder in the face.

The Lyonnais are a tremendous mixture of nationalities. Italian and Spanish names abound, as well as Arabs, Turks and Greeks. The workmen were an example of this. While Bernard Arquillère, the builder, was thoroughly French, his workmen were Turkish, Algerian and Portuguese. Farge the plumber was French, but his employee, Pietri, was of Italian origin. Our tiler, Jean Psaltopoulos, was Greek. Hervé Chichportiche, the painter and decorator, was from north Africa. Jean-Pierre Biancamaria himself is from Corsica. We are English. From somewhere out of this mish-mash of nationalities, unity came, no doubt through Jean-Pierre's efforts. The restaurant, with its white table-cloths, silver chairs, green floor and pink walls, had a definite 'look'. It wasn't French, Italian, Turkish, Spanish or Portuguese. It wasn't even especially British. It was just different.

5

We gave an opening party. It was rather an impromptu affair, since we had not known for sure when the restaurant was going to be ready. I had continued to work in Geneva and elsewhere during the alterations, partly to finance them, and partly to stay out of the way while they were going on. Even after the restaurant was finished I was still in a quandary as to whether to continue working for a few more weeks, or whether to open up immediately. Cold feet inclined me to work as a translator for a while longer, but the clicking of the figures in our bank account after taking the loan we needed suggested opening as soon as possible.

Many decisions about the restaurant seem to have been taken on the spur of the moment, without reflection: the visit to M. Faure, the first trip to the bank, even our arrival in Lyon and the idea of taking over Alain's house. The choice of a name for the restaurant also fell into this 'last minute' category. Two weeks before work finished, I applied myself to the search for a name. Under its layers of table-cloths, one of the Higgins table-tops, which are made of chipboard, is covered with attempts at finding a name. Our ultimate choice may seem simple and, seeing that it's my own name, rather obvious, but we tried out a lot of duds before hitting on it. As a name it functions pretty well: it's short, easy to remember, and has only one letter – the 'H' – that the French have trouble pronouncing. Perhaps most important, since we were to serve British food, it's uncompromisingly British. And it follows the French tradition of naming restaurants after their owners: Paul Bocuse, Alain Chapelle, Pic, Point, Troisgros . . . and now Higgins.

The name went up on the façade of the restaurant shortly before the opening party, which was arranged for a Saturday, and we decided to open officially for business on the following Tuesday, 21 January 1986. For the party we made a token attempt at providing food, and a more serious attempt at providing drink: two barrels of Beaujolais, a lot of bottles of Mâcon Villages and a certain amount of fruit juice. Invitations were made by telephone or simply verbally. We invited friends, and told them to bring their friends. We invited the British community, the British Consul, all the workmen who had worked on the alterations. We invited our family over from Britain, friends from Geneva and, perhaps the best idea of all, we invited people from the street. In fact, I invited absolutely everyone I saw in the street for the two days before the opening. It was good public relations, like inviting neighbours to what are likely to be noisy, late parties, and many of them have become faithful customers and friends since. They might never have tried the restaurant had they not been involved in the inauguration. (The other positive result of our good public relations is that we have very seldom had complaints from the neighbours about noise late at night.)

At the party, we found that large numbers of people were interested in drinking free Beaujolais, despite the fact that the modern Lyonnais has a kind of received mistrust of Beaujolais, due, I think, to a scandal about twenty years ago about the wine being cut with Algerian wine to make it go further. This has since been remedied, but the Lyonnais cling to their antipathy. The restaurant was so crowded it was almost impossible to move. I struggled round, trying to circulate and talk to as many people as possible, but the invitations had got a little out of hand. A photographer friend, Pierre Augros, subsequently to become a favoured customer, stood on a chair in the corner to photograph the room, and thereby nearly caused an incident.

On one of my tours of the room, I came across a couple of fat, moustachioed criminal-looking types who had stationed themselves next to one of the barrels of wine, and were resolutely helping to empty it. At my first encounter with these two, I found myself shaking their hands and being informed that they were a couple of old Croix-Roussiens and that they were extremely glad to be there, just next to an almost unlimited supply of free wine. In my bemused state, I accepted their presence, though I could not imagine who had invited them. About half an hour later, I looked across the room and saw that they were still there, huddled around the barrel, becoming very red in the face. Suddenly I decided that they had been there long enough, so I went over and explained quite firmly that they had not been invited to the opening of my restaurant, and that the door was just behind them. They left muttering curses. Afterwards, the photographer told me that they had approached him and warned him that if any of the photos of them were published in the press, they would return and smash the restaurant. They had hinted at Mafia connections. As it happened, their photos were not published, so their threats were never put to the test. Lyon is supposed to have a powerful Mafia presence – the second in France after Marseilles – but I have never come across it. I was told I might be bothered by protection racketeers requiring contributions (*la pègre* in French), but perhaps my operation is too small to interest them, or perhaps they do not really exist. As for our two uninvited guests, I believe that the amount of wine they had consumed had increased their criminal status in their own eyes, and they were not the godfatherish figures they suggested. I saw them once again, two years later, apparently being forcibly ejected from another Croix-Rousse establishment, so I dare say they made a habit of getting thrown out of places.

The opening party came to an end – most people seemed to think that it had been a success. I was pleased that almost all the workmen who had carried out the alterations had come. Farge was a notable absentee – he was probably worried that we were going to serve tea. I was, in fact, sorry to see the workmen leaving, since it meant that once and for all we had to get down to the business of running the place as a restaurant.

After the party was over, we cleared up the restaurant, arranged a big rectangular table down the centre of the room, and prepared supper for our family and for friends who had come a long way and were staying overnight. In the euphoria induced by what had seemed a successful launch, the pleasure of having so many friends around us and the consumption of a certain quantity of Beaujolais, the actual opening of the restaurant receded into the far distance. Quite understandably, I was distressed to find that my friends were intent on asking me complicated questions of just the type I didn't really want to consider. What was I going to do with the restaurant when it was up and running? How long did I give myself as a restaurateur? And had I thought of what I wanted to do afterwards? What would I do if the thing didn't work? How long would I wait until I decided definitively that it wasn't working, and it was time to pack it in? – in short, the kind of awkward questions that friends can ask simply because they *are* friends. Perhaps the most perilous of all these questions was the highly relevant: what was our first menu to be? How could I possibly be expected to answer this question when I had a full forty-eight hours to go before Tuesday morning? The restaurant had come upon us in a rush, and any problems had been dealt with as they arose, neither thought about before, nor considered much afterwards: the whole thing was so new. True, I had cooked in a couple of restaurants before. True, between us we knew how to cook many different things; but we had never been independent *commer-çants* before, in Britain or in France.

Even the most airy of optimists, and, as they go, I suppose I am pretty airy, must occasionally have moments of doubt about whether things really will turn out all right in the end, and as I lay in bed later that night, I succumbed to just such a moment. Sue, who has a more down-to-earth pessimistic strain, generally manages to balance my optimism, the two opposing characteristics supporting each other. The moments when we both agree that we're heading for catastrophe are dark indeed. Somehow the questions asked at supper had deflated my optimism, and as I lay worrying I thought that Sue might feel the same, and that if I asked the question, her answer would put into words the fear that we had made an almighty mistake. I approached obliquely.

'Are you awake, darling?' I asked, out of the real and spiritual darkness.

'Yes', sleepily.

'You know next Tuesday?'

'Yes'

'Have you thought about what we're going to serve?'

'Yes'

'What did you think of?'

'I thought we'd do chicken and bacon pie and shepherd's pie for lunch, and I thought we'd do smoked trout mousse, mushroom soup, smoked salmon, grapefruit, avocado and chicken salad for starters in the evening, then roast lamb with mint sauce, steak and kidney pie, and that Delia Smith recipe for spicy Indian chicken that I cooked for Katie's twenty-first birthday a few weeks ago. You can do the puddings.'

With all my admiration for my wife, I hadn't expected this. The spiritual part of the darkness started to lighten, but there remained the question that really worried me.

'What'll we do if the restaurant doesn't work? I mean, if it all goes wrong?'

'Oh, you know – we're clever people; we'll change it, do something different with it, find a solution, you'll see. Let's go to sleep now.'

As it always does, Tuesday came around, and we opened up. For our first lunchtime service we did two covers, and for our first evening service we did seven. It was a quiet week that built up to a climax on Friday and Saturday evenings, when a lot of people from the launch party came to eat and we were full. Of course, we were completely exhausted at first, until we got used to the work, or perhaps used to being exhausted, but nevertheless I discovered the intense pleasure of providing a service that people enjoy and appreciate. I also discovered how beautiful the restaurant looked with people in it, talking animatedly at the tables, with a little vase of red roses on each table, the wall lights making the room glow yellow and pink, and the outside floodlights shining through the blue, green and purple glass of the façade windows. I attributed this to Jean-Pierre's skill. To our great pleasure, many of the customers who discovered the restaurant in that first week have remained customers ever since, and they've acquired a status rather similar to that of the original signatories of the Declaration of Independence: '*Nous étions parmi les premiers clients du restau-*

rant', they announce proudly. This I attribute to the fact that there was a sense of adventure in the air about the launch: an English restaurant in Lyon! Will they, or won't they make it? How long will it last? And those first customers, who no doubt wish us well, have accompanied us along the way and are still with us.

6

Perhaps one of the nicest things about owning a restaurant is choosing what you are going to serve in it. In our case, we decided that the menu would be small and that we would make use of no frozen or tinned produce at all. We would, in fact, dispense with the use of a freezer altogether. This philosophy springs from a distrust of restaurants offering a comprehensive overview of almost every item in the international cuisine repertoire, and we have stuck to it since. Freezer-to-microwave cooking exists everywhere, even in France, but I feel that if people want to eat frozen food, then they can do so at home. A trip to a restaurant, necessarily something of a luxury, should be a pleasurable experience. The other day, looking round a professional kitchen equipment showroom, I found a gleaming stainless steel unit which contained fridge, freezer and microwave, all in one. Inside the freezer were rows and rows of shallow trays, which could be lifted out and slotted immediately into racks in the microwave, requiring nothing more than a certain minimal manual dexterity on the part of the cook, or rather, technician.

In France, the availability of good produce is astonishing. Whereas in Britain it might be hard to obtain daily supplies of fresh meat, vegetables, fish, cheese, might indeed be harder still to find someone to deliver this produce every day to your door, in France this poses no problem. We were helped in our choice of suppliers by another friend and well-known Lyon restaurateur, Sylvain Roiret. When our project started to materialize, Sylvain opened up his little notebook, and revealed about ten years of research to us. He even did it with a good grace. After all, we were not in the same area of town – his restaurant is right in the centre, the heart of the Presqu'île – nor are we at all the same sort of restaurant.

Approaching suppliers through an already established and well-known restaurateur, especially one from the Roiret family, who are pillars of Lyon's old bourgeoisie, was a great advantage. Thus La Société Rhodanienne des Viandes was chosen in preference to La Grande Boucherie du Nord or La Grande Boucherie Centrale. La Rhodanienne are occasional suppliers of meat to Bocuse, high priest of French food, to Léon de Lyon, the Bistrot de Lyon, Sylvain and countless other large, small, well-known or unknown establishments, ranging from the roughest bistro to the smartest gastronomic palace. It is a family firm with about thirty employees, working in continuous shifts from five in the morning till half-past seven at night, with a mere three hours' lunch break, when they realize they would have no customers anyway.

La Rhodanienne's headquarters is in the Halles Centrales, Lyon's main retail food market. This used to be housed in an attractive 19th-century building, with much glass and wrought-iron work, right in the centre of town. These premises became too small, and the Halles moved to the edge of the awful Part Dieu area, into an extremely ugly concrete building. But the suppliers are so marvellous that the surroundings hardly matter, and besides, the stalls themselves are beautiful. Arriving early in the morning, you will see the stallholders spraying their lettuce jungles with a fine spray of water – clumps of brown and white oak-leaf lettuces, tufts of curly endive, bushes of lollo rosso, cress, rocket, lamb's lettuce, young dandelion leaves, spinach – and polishing fruit and vegetables and arranging them in shining piles. Beans from Kenya, raspberries from Chile, cranberries from the USA, passion fruit from God knows where, but not a lot of stuff from Britain. Not a Bramley apple in sight, nor a Cox's Orange Pippin, though plenty of Granny Smiths and not very appetizing Golden Delicious can be had, and for cooking, Reine de Reinettes or Canada Grise apples are not bad.

The next stall may be selling *foie gras*, smoked salmon, caviare, smoked *magret de canard*, bottles of Sauternes, champagne or luxury chocolates. On the left of the Halles, near the entrance, is Goguillot, a marvellous fishmonger, whose fish are always beautifully laid out on crushed ice: pink langoustines, red mullet, trout, monkfish (never with their heads, which are so ugly it would stop people from wanting to eat them), wings of skate, mussels, *coquilles Saint-Jacques*, scallops, squid, and underneath, at foot level, tanks of live fish, trout and pike, lobsters and crayfish, looking like creatures from another planet.

Further on is Maréchal, cheese merchant, with another beautiful stall. Set out on the counter are numerous rush-lined basket trays, with little pieces of cheese skewered on toothpicks for you to taste. Maréchal even hands out glasses of wine for you to try as well. It must be said that his prices are high enough to pay for what would otherwise be excessive generosity. Cheese is expensive stuff in France, too. Maréchal has been known to stock Stilton and even the odd Cheddar, but the quality has never been up to that of his Roquefort, Fourme d'Ambert, Bleu d'Auvergne, or Comté. I have sometimes felt that those cheese merchants in France who occasionally stock British cheeses do so in order to convince their customers that there is absolutely no point at all in buying them. One particular horror I have seen from time to time is 'Top Hole Cheddar', an orange monstrosity wrapped in red wax like a Dutch cheese. Talking of which, the French seem quite able to take Edam and Gouda seriously, so why not Double Gloucester and farmhouse Cheddar? Good Cheddar and Stilton rank among the finest cheeses in the world, but when you start to mention them to the French, they adopt a most annoying attitude. A highly irritating, knowing smile spreads across their faces, for they know that they are in the unassailable position of world supremacy as far as cheese is concerned: no country can equal France in terms of variety and quality. But this does not mean that other countries' products might not be very good indeed.

'*Ah oui,*' they say when mention is made of Cheddar, smile firmly in place, '*le Chester*'. But what is Chester? They don't mean Cheshire – I know, because I have asked them on numerous occasions. At some stage in the past twenty years or so, a company must have carried out an enormous advertising campaign to promote a no doubt dreadful cheese called 'Chester' – and this is what the French know about British cheese. 'Top Hole' cheese may very well be the same product under a different name. I persist in the belief that it is all part of the French Dairy Board's attempt to convince the public that British produce is rubbish. At a recent trade fair in Lyon's Palais des Expositions, the 'Salon de Métiers de Bouche' (tricky to translate, that, but further proof that the French are mouth fetishists), there was a small, rather apologetic stall for, I think, the British Milk Marketing Board. The Salon lasted about a week, and I visited it on two occasions, on the second of which I managed to locate this stall. It was hot in the exhibition halls – many thousands of people visited the show daily – and the refrigeration unit on this stall had broken down earlier in the week and had not been repaired. The cheese was all going rotten. It looked as if it might not have been too bad to begin with, but now the Stiltons had great grey cracks in them, from which the fat was oozing in a most unappetizing way. The Cheddars were perspiring freely, while oddities such as Sage Derby had acquired that glazed, plastic appearance that they adopt when rather too warm. I could only suspect sabotage. At the suggestion of the woman on the stall, I left my name and address, just in case the French end of this British operation might be interested in selling one of their unrotten items occasionally, but was never contacted.

Initially we had our cheeses sent to us directly from Britain. They came from Chewton Cheese Dairy Farm, in Somerset. The sales manager assured us that there would be no problem at all in sending supplies out to France, and that the ordinary postal service could be used. I admit I had slight doubts about the legality of this operation, since normally foodstuffs have to be transported under rigorous conditions, with hygiene certificates supplied by the transporters. They also have to pass through customs, via a forwarding agent, and this my cheeses from Somerset never did. But the main problem was that the packaging did not adequately protect the cheeses and, once broken, a Stilton goes off very rapidly. They would regularly arrive cracked and, since their journey had not been a properly refrigerated one, sometimes smelling strongly of ammonia. The Cheddar fared better than the softer Stilton, but was less appreciated by the French, anyway. On one last occasion, I was telephoned by the local post office and told in terms of outrage that unless I came to collect an evil-smelling parcel within the next hour, it would be deposited directly in the dustbin. I had thought that the French were used to high-smelling cheeses. Well, high-smelling cheeses, yes, but not high-smelling parcels. It was true that on this occasion the cheese was not in a good state. Then there were difficulties with the farm's receptionist and secretary to Mrs Clarke, the sales manager. In an attempt to keep my phone bill to a minimum, I would try to be as brisk as possible when ringing Chewton to pass an order:

'Good morning,' I would say briskly, 'Tom Higgins here. I'm calling from Lyon in France. I wonder if I could speak to Mrs Clarke, please?' Then, very slowly, a voice with a light West Country accent would reply,

'Good morning.' (Long pause.) 'Chewton Cheese Dairy Farm.' (Pause.) 'Can I help you?'

'Yes' (more briskly still), 'it's Tom Higgins from Lyon. I'd like to talk to Mrs Clarke, please.'

(Pause.) 'Who did you say was calling?'

'Tom Higgins' (astonishingly briskly), 'from Lyon. Mrs Clarke, please.'

'Lyon in France, is that?'

'Yes' (briskness now verging on rage), 'that's right. Now if I could just speak to Mrs Clarke.'

'I'll just go and see if she's in her office.' (Pause.) 'Would you mind just repeating your name again please?' In retrospect it occurred to me that this was probably very loyal protection of the no doubt overworked Mrs Clarke – a kind of telephonic 'screening', to eliminate time-wasters. At all events, my nerves were not up to it. Consequently a new supplier was sought and found: an importer in the Rungis wholesale market in Paris is able to provide Stiltons and Cheddars which are, on the whole, of very good quality, sometimes absolutely top class. On rare occasions I have even been sent Chewton cheeses, so the importer obviously knows his stuff.

Back in the Halles, and pressing further in towards the

centre, you may come to one of the oyster bars, its counters glistening darkly with *fruits de mer*. Rows and rows of prehistoric-looking, encrusted, *fines claires*, (oysters) of different sizes are laid out on crushed ice, along with piles of spiky black sea-urchins, mussels and clams of various sorts. A certain amount of imported and artistically arranged seaweed completes the maritime, octopus's garden appearance of these stalls. Behind the counter, in a room partitioned off from the alleyways of the Halles in wood and opaque glass, rather like a very large, old-fashioned railway compartment, there is just space for about twenty-five very tightly packed people to sit and eat their *assiettes de fruits de mer*, the seafood sitting on crushed ice on a kind of multistorey wire tower. Served with very thin slices of brown bread and butter, quarters of lemon (essential for testing oysters) and, if you are rich, washed down with a bottle of champagne, a couple of dozen *fines claires* will set you back about 400 francs. If you are not feeling so rich, the same oysters, with a bottle of Muscadet, that light, dry and relatively humble wine from the Atlantic end of the Loire which goes so well with seafood, will cost about 250 francs. I enjoy the idea of oysters, like all the fuss made about them – the tower they are served on, the crushed ice and the seaweed – but in fact I can never manage to eat more than six, which makes me a relatively economical person to invite to an oyster-bar. Eating cheek-to-jowl, with conversation all round at maximum decibels, oyster consumption in the Halles is an interesting experience that is not to everyone's taste, but should be tried at least once.

A few steps further in and you arrive at La Rhodanienne.

Not a lot of effort has been put into making the stall attractive; it is lit up in white, orange and red neon, rather like a fairground shooting gallery. Piles of different cuts of meat are laid out in refrigerated glass cabinets. At one end of the stall are cooked meats, pâtés, sausages and a formidable quantity of *andouillettes* – fat sausages which seem to me to be a French version of haggis. (La Rhodanienne can also supply basic cooked dishes such as a *cassoulet* or *tripes à la mode de Caën*, a dish of tripe baked for hours in a sealed pot with homely vegetables like carrots and onions.) Slabs of meat in large quantities are not for the faint-hearted and La Rhodanienne cannot be described as ideal sightseeing material. It is essentially a supplier for professional customers, and the public retail side of the business is less important than the restaurant side. Behind the counter you can see through glass partitions into the inner sanctum or workshop area, where at any given time eight or ten extremely gory butchers are hacking at enormous carcasses with cleavers, hatchets, BIG knives, saws, or even more nightmarish, using a kind of wall-mounted jig-saw to cut shinbones into chunks (for use in *fond de veau* (veal stock), for example). Even the most hardened meat-lover is likely to see the point of vegetarianism a little more clearly after a trip to La Rhodanienne.

La Rhodanienne delivers daily all round Lyon, and is lucky to have one of the nicest delivery-men in the town, Manu. Trilingual product of a Portuguese mother and an Italian father, Manu talks French with a very strong Lyonnais accent. He serves as a kind of central newsagency for a certain circle of restaurateurs, bringing news of trade in

other areas of town and messages from other establishments, and taking on news to his next port of call. Some
years ago, out walking with Alain Ville, we spotted a shop-
owner that we knew, standing disconsolately in the doorway of his shop, which sold hats. '*Comment vas-tu?*' called
Alain.

'*Pas très bien*', replied the man, 'business is much too
quiet.' Then, brightening a little: 'But apparently it's the
same everywhere.' When I heard this, I determined on two
things. The first was not to associate myself so closely with
my business that when someone asked me how I was, I
automatically replied for the restaurant, as though we were
one and the same thing. The second was never to hide
behind the idea that trade was bad for me, simply because it
was bad everywhere. 'I am fine,' I imagined myself replying
blithely to enquiries after my health, 'but business is lousy.
No,' I would continue, 'business is booming everywhere, it's
just here that there's nobody, they've all decided to stay
away from here, that's all.' Now, eight years later, I realize
how difficult this is for a small business. The restaurant is so
personal that it *is* my life, and when it is going badly, it has
an effect on how I feel – I do feel less well. When we are full
all the time, even if the work is tremendously tiring, I feel
much better. Consequently, with all my good, strong-
minded resolutions, I am there with all the other restaurateurs, at the door, waiting for Manu, relieved to find that
no establishment similar to my own is going well, that so-
and-so has ordered no meat for a week, that another has
only taken eight lamb-chops since Tuesday. Manu, although a truthful harbinger of tidings from afar, is also a

consummate diplomat, and while he may be capable of saying that the centre of town is booming while my restaurant is empty, he will always apply therapeutic treatment afterwards, saying that the Croix-Rousse is quiet all over, that it is only restaurants with terraces that are busy, that people are eating nothing but fish, *choucroûte* (sauerkraut), steak and chips, *andouillettes*, that the latest craze is tapas bars, Tex-Mex food, Greek or Turkish food, hamburgers, restaurants where you can dance, cocktail bars giving light snacks or sandwiches, Moroccan, Tunisian or Lebanese food, or any one of the innumerable gimmicky, gim-crack, passing fancies that can, momentarily, only on a temporary basis, distract customers away from the one, correct and honest path, along which lie the restaurants which toil away at serving good solid meals. Like us.

7

When the restaurant first opened we had no car. We had in fact sold one (a much missed convertible Triumph) to purchase a fridge. For a while I began to acquire a reputation as one of the only restaurateurs in Lyon who fetched his supplies by metro and bus, but this was quickly abandoned, since carrying 15 kilos of meat, 4 kilos of fish and a lot of vegetables on crowded public transport is not at all easy. The result was that almost all our food had to be delivered to us. For some time, therefore, our vegetables were brought to us by a company called Chazot, whose base was in the wholesale market, the Marché Gare. The disadvantage with Chazot was that, except in certain specific cases – bananas, parsley, cucumber and so on, you were obliged to order by the crate. Trays of lettuce, courgettes and cauliflower would linger sadly in the cellar or in our alleyway, since the consumption of the restaurant in its early days was not sufficient to cope with such quantities.

The technique was the same as for La Rhodanienne. At night, at the end of the service, a message would be left with Chazot and the following day a lorry, driven with all the verve of the French Peugeot rally team, would come careering up to the door. I became enormously sensitive to the particular noise made by the Chazot lorry and was able to distinguish its approach from that of other, similar vehicles. The driver, an irrepressibly cheerful and amiable young man, looked as though he spent his entire free time fighting. Every day he would arrive with some new and even more hideous scar or lump on his face. Finally he turned up with an eye-patch over his left eye and announced that he had been in a car-crash and had '*perdu mon oeil*' – or at least, that was what we thought he said, but his extremely strong Lyonnais accent, coupled with what appeared to be a sort of explosive speech impediment, overlaid with the damage sustained to his lower face during the terrible drubbing he seemed to have taken the previous night, made understanding him very tricky. It turned out, however, that he had indeed lost his eye, and ever after we used to refer to him as 'purdoohmonoye'. Chazot's produce was very good, and if ever there was anything that was not acceptable, they would change it the following day. However, they had one slightly vexatious habit. The day after the receipt of their monthly account, it was not 'purdoohmonoye' who would turn up to collect payment, but three extremely aggressive-looking men. I felt this indicated a lack of confidence not justified in my case.

All dry stock – seasoning, flour, sugar, cleaning products, oil and so on – were supplied originally by a company called Pérache S.A. Again, the service was first class and the delivery man uncomplaining at having to carry the goods up to the second floor of our house, where I originally stored them in what used to be a derelict apartment. Many of the goods were heavy – cases of 12 litres of oil, or packs of 500 paper table-cloths, for example, so I used to dread the deliveries from Pérache, since I felt obliged to help unload the lorry and take the stock upstairs. Now I have made a lot of shelving space downstairs at street level, so unloading from the street is no longer so awful.

In any case both Chazot and Pérache have now been ousted by Metro, an enormous cash-and-carry in Vaulx-en-Velin, a rather dreary urban area on the outskirts of the city. I suppose that it is sad to abandon small, private companies for a huge, anonymous supplier, but it must be admitted that Metro is awfully good. I recently took an English restaurateur there, and he was absolutely astonished at the quality and variety of the goods on offer – infinitely superior, he said, to anything equivalent in Britain. At Metro, you can take one of the big trolleys and circulate among the shelving as at a supermarket. These trolleys are about 7 feet long, and during the first few weeks of opening, when customers had not got the hang of how to manoeuvre them, they made Metro a fairly hazardous place, as dozens of utterly out-of-control trolleys careered helplessly around.

The chief advantage of Metro is that everything is under one roof. One single bill replaces a multitude of small bills that would otherwise have had to be individually entered into the books. There is a huge and very chilly section for fresh vegetables and fruit, which come from all over the world. It is possible, though expensive, to have fresh raspberries in February, red-currants in January, or grapes in April, not to mention the constant availability of the inedible exotica which look so spectacular in fruit-bowls and of which I do not even know the names. There is an equally vast section for dairy produce, cheese, and such products as *foie gras*, smoked cods' roe and smoked *magret de canard*, a section for cooked meats, a huge butcher's shop, bank after bank of frozen goods, and a fresh fish area, with tanks of live lobsters, crabs, trout and pike. Then there are rows and rows of shelves covering everything from tomato purée to an extensive range of malt whiskies. And that is less than half the shop. The other half is given over to a display of kitchen equipment: fridges, stoves, cold-stores, slicers and whizzers in general, coffee machines and so on. Then there are plates, knives, glasses, ashtrays, jugs, champagne-stoppers, boiled-egg slicers and innumerable other esoteric objects. You can dress your chefs and your waiters, provide towels and bedding, if you have a hotel, buy tables, chairs and cupboards, music systems, televisions, videos. In short, it would be possible to equip totally a restaurant or hotel from this one shop.

Purchasing on a small scale, or of very perishable products like lettuces, is undertaken at the local street market, the Marché de la Croix-Rousse. This, as I mentioned earlier, is one of the most remarkable in Lyon, and certainly one of the biggest. It is really two separate markets which are not quite joined together. One part, about 200 metres from where we live, fills the Petite Place de la Croix-Rousse, a square of rather plain but attractive early 19th-century houses. This is the part we use most, since it is so near to us, but it is a good deal more expensive than the main market, which stretches for almost a kilometre along the wide, tree-lined Boulevard de la Croix-Rousse. In our small section, the range of stalls is relatively limited – there are about eight stalls selling vegetables and fruit, one stall selling flowers, and our cheese and dairy suppliers, Gérard and Marie Imbert. Then on certain days there are additional stalls selling meat, charcuterie, honey and more cheese. If we need some slightly unusual product for the restaurant, such as herbs other than thyme, bay or rosemary – dill or sage, for example – then we have to find them in the big market. There, one can also buy game, *volaille* (chicken, ducks, geese, guinea fowl), rabbit, hare, fish, kitchen utensils and all manner of surprising things.

The market is very beautiful, and it is a pleasure to go to. However, although it is near, it cannot really be called very convenient. The space the small market occupies in the middle of the square is relatively narrow, and on important market days when there are a lot of stalls (Tuesday, Saturday and Sunday), the passageway between them resembles a highly coloured pathway through a vegetable jungle. Imagine a tunnel roofed in by the canvas stall covers on either side, giving the light in the market a curious, sub-aquatic quality. Then imagine the walls of the tunnel, built with tray upon tray of different sorts of lettuces – red, brown, white, green, the leaves wide and flat, frilly, crinkled or in fern-like fronds – all sorts of vegetables, overflowing trays of grapes in autumn, piles of strawberries and raspberries in summer. Imagine the smell of earth, moist vegetables, fruit, cheese and flowers, and the cries of stall-holders, each trying to draw the attention of the passing customer. Now, imagine the passing customers themselves. It may just be an illusion, but most shoppers appear to be elderly, bulky women and, the market being a convivial place, the Croix-Rousse locals like to meet each other there and spend a few minutes chatting. They may also know the stall-holders, some of whom have been coming to the same spot every day for the last forty years. Anyway, this narrow tunnel, packed with highly voluble, large, generally female individuals chatter-ing amongst themselves, but nonetheless keeping an eye on the stall-holders to ascertain that they are served in order, presents a formidable barrier. Remember also that each of these shoppers is, as you are yourself, encumbered with a capacious basket or shopping trolley, and you will realize that it is almost impossible to pierce a rapid passage through the market.

It is for this reason that I encourage Sue to make the daily trip to the market. At the risk of allowing a wholly inap-propriate sexist element to enter this narrative, it appears to me that, as market-goers, women are superior to men. At any rate, Sue is a good deal more efficient than I am in the market. The one stall-holder she more or less refuses to deal with is Charly, the flower merchant. Charly has been on the market for close on thirty years and, since he is a wholesale dealer at the Marché Gare, is immensely rich already. The only reason he appears every day on the Marché de la Croix-Rousse is because he loves it. He is what the French refer to as *une grande gueule*, which basically means 'loud-mouth', and his mouth certainly is a loud one. All morning he maintains a constant stream of slightly risqué patter, commenting on passers-by, politics and the weather, or sounding off his personal philosophy. He uses the familiar '*tu*' with everybody and expects them to use it back to him. His shout ''IGGINS – 'OW YOU DO-DOOO?' echoes round the entire square 50 metres before we arrive at his stall. It took me three years to realize that he was trying to say 'How do you do?', his last faint vestige of school English. He sells magnificent flowers, cheaper than elsewhere and far cheaper than they would be in Britain. On days when other flower merchants put up their prices as they know that demand will be high – St Valentine's day, or All Souls' day, when the French deck out the graves of their departed family – Charly's prices remain at the same level as usual. Away from his flower stall, he is an utterly different character. On the occasions when he has come to the restaurant, there has been no shouting, no loud jokes, no blue humour; he has been the soul of quiet, well-behaved discretion.

Of all our suppliers, the ones with whom we have established the closest friendship are the Imberts, who provide us with dairy produce. They often visit the restaurant; we have been to their house, gone on picnics together (provided by them and quite magnificent), and lunched together. Gérard and I share a birthday, and he is keen to point out that we have the same character (anxiety-ridden Virgos, both). He has now been supplying us with Cheddar and Stilton – obtained from Rungis Market in Paris – for about eight years, and he is still unable to pronounce the word 'Stilton', which he thinks is 'Schilton'. I could obtain most of the produce I get from Gérard at Metro, and it would certainly be cheaper. Then I think of the pleasure of dealing with such nice people, the advantage of having them two minutes' walk away every morning, the certainty that the produce is absolutely fresh, and I decide not to change.

In the beginning we were so daunted by the problems with fish that we did not serve it at all. I was worried that unless it was used instantly it would go off. However, if stored properly, fish will last almost as well as meat in a refrigerator, although ideally it likes to sit on crushed ice at around 2 degrees centigrade. Now we always have a fish dish, as well as several fishy starters. Initially, we purchased our supplies from a certain M. Duvier, whose shop was on the Boulevard de la Croix-Rousse, about fifteen minutes' walk from the restaurant. Duvier's shop 'La Marée Fraîche', was a kind of permanent stall, with a refrigerated lock-up and a cold counter that could be wheeled out on to the pavement when the shop was open, and locked away inside when closed. Duvier and his wife, both perfectly pleasant, adopted a nautical style of dress appropriate to their trade: big, roll-neck sweaters with anchor motifs, wellington boots, Breton fishermen's hats, sou'westers and so on. They were both sorely afflicted by M. Duvier's aged mother, a very determined old woman who clearly refused to retire. Duvier's dealings with his customers, during which he wore a half toothless and, it must be admitted, not altogether convincing smile, were constantly punctuated, as he tried to keep his mother under control, by cries of '*Non maman, tu touches pas ça*', '*Mais non maman, je te dis, ne fais pas ça*', '*Arrètes, tais-toi maman*', and even, I'm afraid, '*Qu'est-ce-qu'elle m'emmerde, cette vielle*'. Duvier's mother took all this philosophically; she was more than a trifle deaf and perhaps did not even hear some of the harsher imprecations. Often she was too busy regaling customers with tales of some of the more awful illnesses which afflicted her. She also wore nautical accoutrements: a kind of long, green, rubberized cape, tied at the waist with a World War I belt, and a head scarf fastened tightly under her chin, and to my eye she resembled nothing so much as an old trout, or perhaps an old cod. Certainly she could not be described as an ornament to the stall.

I was initially attracted to 'La Marée Fraîche' by the sight of a tray of what I took to be genuine English smoked haddock: thick, pale golden fillets of fish, with the skin still in place. I mentioned this to Duvier and he assured me that the product did indeed come from England. Afterwards, he would pin a notice on the fish saying '*Haddok anglais*' (sic), since he became convinced that this was a selling point. Excellent smoked haddock is produced in Bordeaux, but otherwise the French product sometimes tends to be over-salted and artificially coloured. Things went all right for a while, though we noticed that the unlucky Duvier seemed to have fewer and fewer customers. Then, suddenly, three times in short succession, he supplied us with bad fish. On one occasion I took some fish that he recommended and found it to be unusable when we got home. Of course, he changed it, but our relationship had become strained and shortly afterwards we moved to Bozzo, a fishmonger who is much nearer our house and who maintains the highest possible standards, but who is undeniably expensive. At the moment it looks as though Metro, with its gigantic fish counters, will win us away, at least partially, from Bozzo.

The French attach a huge importance to bread as an accompaniment to meals. A recent restaurant review I read praised a well-known establishment (Le Nandron, in the centre of town, one Michelin star), for the special care it took in matching different types of bread to the different courses of a meal, so as to be absolutely certain that the sensual gastronomic pleasure of each mouthful never fell below fever pitch: *pain de seigle* served with goat's cheese, *pain de campagne* with robust, rustic stews, *pain de noix* with smoked fish, a hefty loaf with plenty of crumb for meat dishes, thinner loaves with more crust for fish and so on. (My feelings about providing different sorts of bread with each course is that once you get beyond a certain point such attention to detail is merely symptomatic of the hysteria surrounding Lyonnais gastronomy.) The French dedication to bread is shown by the extraordinary number of bakeries in each area. On a quick count, there are seven bakeries within 300 metres of the restaurant and this is not counting shops which are primarily pâtisseries, but which produce a bit of bread as a sideline.

Mme Renard, who owns the main bakery in our part of the Croix-Rousse, provides us with bread. The shop is beautiful and spotlessly clean, the service good and the quality almost always very high. Basically we buy only two sorts of bread: long, crusty white French loaves weighing 500g each, known as '*flutes*' in Lyon, but as '*baguettes*' in Paris (a '*baguette*' in Lyon is, I believe, called a '*ficelle*' in Paris, and is a much thinner, lighter loaf); and a slightly coarse brown loaf, which we have sliced up for us on a Heath-Robinson like machine with a lot of jiggling vertical blades. Mme Renard and her staff went in for a good deal of public relations activity in order to secure the Higgins custom. This mostly involved making a tremendous fuss of Xavier when we brought him into the shop. Mme Renard made considerable efforts to learn a bit of English, though the boy resolutely refuses to talk English to anyone who is clearly French. She got to the stage when she could say 'Good morning' and 'Good afternoon', but was unable to remember which meant which. Xavier quickly understood, as is the way with young human beings, that he had only to smile or, at the most, give Mme Renard a kiss, and he would walk away clutching an assortment of biscuits in his chubby little hands.

Mme Renard is an excellent businesswoman, and her bakery, run formerly with her husband, but now with her son, who supervises the baking, is quite a big business, and must employ around fifteen people. She is small, solidly built and dark, with a very piercing gaze, and speaks her mind with unnerving frankness. On one occasion I remember feeling deep sympathy for some poor biscuit representative who had called in to find out how one of his new products was doing. Mme Renard was giving a precise resumé of her total disdain for it (I believe that of the three packets sold, two had been returned as unsatisfactory.) The man was clearly hoping that the floor would open and that he could plunge downwards into the welcoming darkness. Mme Renard is hard as nails in business, and her love of money is legendary on the Plateau de la Croix-Rousse; but then, her produce is very good and she works exceedingly hard, so I feel she deserves her success. One member of her staff, Yvette, clearly disapproves of the hefty profit margin, however, and plays a kind of Russian roulette, with her employer as the loaded pistol. Whenever we buy croissants or cakes from Yvette, we find that either more than we ordered has been popped into the bag, or too much change has been returned to us. For example, 20 francs is handed over for a purchase costing 16 francs 40. A great deal of muttering ensues: '*Allons-voir, vingt francs moins seize quarante, ça fait, ça fait, ça fait trois soixante. Voilà Monsieur Higgins, ça fait vingt.*' But instead of 3 francs 60, 10 francs are pressed conspiratorally into my hand. And this under the eagle eye of Mme Renard herself. When the shop is full and there are two lines of people in front of the counter, and Mme Renard and Yvette are serving, the Yvette queue is always significantly longer than the Renard queue.

Once I arrived late in the evening to fetch bread for the restaurant, having forgotten it earlier. Three members of the Renard staff were behind the counter and the shop was empty. Mme Renard was in the back room, visible through an open door, counting her money. Three *flutes* remain on the shelves, and several other varieties of bread.

'*Ça tombe bien,*' I said, '*Je prends les trois flutes qui restent.*' Perfectly in time, the three women began to shake their heads at me, at the same time glancing nervously through the open door to see if 'la Renard' was watching them. I realized that this bread was not the freshest available from the shop, and had in fact remained unsold from the day before. I was directed to another sort of bread. Sometimes I feel that the whole thing is an elaborate public relations exercise planned by Mme Renard herself, exhibiting an extraordinary grasp of the image she presents to the public, and that Yvette is her accomplice and instructed to hand out a certain amount of free food every day.

Renard's shop is 200 metres from the restaurant, on the corner of the Place de la Croix-Rousse. Bozzo's shop is almost opposite the bakery, and Gérard and Marie's stall is 20 metres further on, with Charly the flower merchant's stall just beyond. A typical trip to the market involves calling at all these places, gradually filling a large basket with goods, assembling a collection of plastic bags in the other hand, then struggling home to the restaurant, invariably to find that the keys are buried at the bottom of the basket, under bread, under lettuce, under flowers, fruit, cream and butter, under fish.

8

We had a very limited wine-list in the early days of the restaurant – just one Côtes du Rhône, a Beaujolais Villages, a Bordeaux and a white Mâcon. This kind of approach is relatively common with small Lyonnais restaurants who wish to keep things as simple as possible. Maintaining a hefty wine-list over a period of years, changing from one vintage to another, being able to supply half bottles if required, making sure that the cellar is in order, that the stock is not lying too long in the restaurant, that everything is more or less at the right temperature, is an extremely arduous business; hence the employment by large restaurants of a *sommelier* (wine-waiter), whose job it is to look after all such details. Nevertheless, over the years our wine-list has grown slowly, and we now have about twenty-five wines on offer. Rather than choosing simply the best-known names, whose fame obviously adds to the price of the bottle, our aim has been to seek excellence a little further down the scale: providing what we consider to be a first-class Côtes de Blaye, for example, instead of a mediocre Saint-Emilion. Rather than opting for a Côtes Rôtie, which would cost us 150 francs a bottle, and would have to appear on the wine-list at well over 300 francs (we wouldn't sell a single bottle), we have far more reasonably priced wines from Tulette, Beaumes-de-Venise and Vaqueyras. Similarly, top quality Gigondas from the bottom end of the Côtes du Rhône will not cost as much as an equivalent Saint-Joseph from the northern end, opposite Vienne, but to my mind, the southern wine is more interesting.

It is not really feasible for a restaurant to sell wine costing a great deal more than one of its menus. Since our most expensive menu is 125 francs, we cannot sell bottles of wine at more than 140 francs. Thus, our most expensive bottles are an absolutely delicious Moulin-à-Vent which we sell for 115 francs, a beautiful Chablis at 125 francs, and a Marques de Riscal Rioja which we sell with difficulty, since it's something of an oddity for the French, at 135 francs. Almost all our wines have been chosen by us on our visits to producers or *négociants* (merchants) in the various districts, the exceptions being those areas further from Lyon, like Bordeaux, Cahors and Champagne. These latter I have bought principally at wine fairs.

Wine is a marvellous product. It comes in so many different forms. Even the bottles are beautiful, and I confess I am much addicted to having my cellar as full as possible, simply because the racks look so wonderful filled with bottles, their necks dusty or gleaming in the dim light of the vaulted rooms. On the other hand, I have to be careful not to put too much money into the cellar, thereby immobilizing working capital. From this point of view, it is a good thing that the cellar is not very big – we keep a stock of about 500 bottles, quite sufficient for a small restaurant, and use only two rooms of its potential four, which measure about 10 feet by 8 feet and about 10 feet square. The cellar itself lies immediately below the restaurant, but without direct access to it. Consequently, when a bottle is required during the service, I have to go out into the street, then back into the house via the (massively bolted) alley door.

Down in the cellar, all is calm. The temperature remains constant throughout the hottest summer and the coldest winter. There is silence. The floor is simply beaten earth, which apparently is the best thing for cellar floors, since it maintains the level of humidity required to stop the corks in the bottles from drying out. The walls, which are made of honey-coloured stone from the Beaujolais, the *pierre dorée* of so many lower Burgundian farmhouses and cottages, give the impression of immense antiquity; they look Roman, at the very least. What I would like to have in my cellar is a marble table in the middle, with a wooden cutting-board on it, a couple of knives, some glasses and a bottle opener – the latter sensibly attached to a useful hook with some string, so that such an indispensable tool should never go missing. There would be a couple of chairs or stools, and some *saucisson* suspended from the ceiling, easily reachable from the stools, enabling slices to be cut off with the aforementioned knives on the aforementioned cutting-board. Other provisions might include a little cheese, some bread and perhaps some salted almonds or olives. It would then be possible to pass many a pleasant moment in the cellar with a friend of one's choice, absently reaching for another bottle in the racks just next to one, should the need for such a thing arise.

What prevents me from realizing this scheme is the time-switch on the cellar lights. This provides four minutes of light before automatically cutting out. Even in full daylight, very little light filters down into the depths of the cellar, and at night the pitchy blackness is absolute. To be caught in the back room by the automatic cut-out is not an agreeable experience. Well, you may say, why not have the light system altered, surely not such a tricky thing to arrange? I think that what we have here is a case of the flesh, albeit weak, recognizing the wisdom of not touching an electrical system which preserves one from the folly of evenings, afternoons and possibly even mornings of debauchery spent in a wine-cellar with a bottle opener to hand.

Choosing wine to fill this cellar, and keeping it stocked, is one of the nicest parts of our job, not simply because wine is such an interesting subject, but also because the places where it is made tend to be beautiful. One of our first moves when confronted with the empty cellar six years ago was to drive to Belleville, a small town in the Beaujolais which does not belie its name, since it is indeed a pretty place. It has a magnificent Romanesque church, the tower a stack of delicate rounded arches, one main street about 2 kilometres long, and another, less important street at right angles to this. It's about the size of an English market town. We went in search of a company called Vins Dessalle, which has supplied the restaurant with many excellent wines over the last few years. This company has now moved to larger premises, but its earlier buildings had far more character. It used to be housed in a high, iron warehouse, purpose-built in the 19th century and now covered with a creeper of some sort. The offices were in a wooden and glass structure adjacent to the warehouse. The latter was filled on one side with cases of wine stacked up on shelves to the ceiling, 20 feet high, and on the other side were the great *fûts* (barrels) of wine from the different areas of the Beaujolais. I suppose it must be considered a good thing that not everybody in Britain knows that it is possible to get free wine from every wine producer in wine-growing areas, on the pretext of tasting with a view to purchase. The vineyards would be permanently flooded with drunken Britons, the roads littered with the inevitable crashes of their vehicles. The reputation of '*la perfide Albion*' would sink drastically.

When tasting wine, it is perhaps an unfortunate, but nonetheless absolute necessity to make use of the *crachoir* that the producer provides more or less automatically, to enable his customers to avoid excessive consumption of alcohol. The *crachoir* may be a simple bucket, filled with wood-shavings; it may be a special basin – in Sylvain Fessy's new premises, tasting is carried out around a very smart little copper sink, which stands, rather like a font, in the middle of the room; or it may just be a gutter, which can be sluiced clean with water, running down the centre of the wine-store, as it was in M. Fessy's last premises.

I am now capable of performing the rigmarole of wine tasting. I can hold the glass up to the light to gauge its colour, swirl it round to see how it clings to the sides of the glass, sniff at it to judge its 'nose', and sip it and keep the liquid on my tongue while trying to isolate the various tastes that may appear – raspberry, strawberry, nut, apple and so on. I can keep the wine on the top of my tongue and breathe air in through my mouth making the sort of slurping noise we got into such trouble for making when we were children. This particular activity enables you to judge the alcohol content of the wine, since it takes the fumes of alcohol straight up your nose. I can expel the wine from my mouth in a concentrated spurt, generally getting it into the *crachoir*. After this, the practice is to adopt a ruminative expression, as you wait to see how long the taste of the wine will remain in your mouth, and what happens to it as it stays there – does a sudden acidity or harshness present itself, for example

But at our level all this palaver is a little beside the point. These days, when I purchase wine, I have two criteria. The most important is whether or not I like it, and frankly, when you are not very expert, indeed have only a very little knowledge, all that business of sorting the different flavours out on the various parts of your palate sometimes stops you from considering whether or not you are enjoying the taste of the wine. The question I ask myself is whether the wine is the sort I would like to drink in a restaurant at such and such a price. The second criterion is whether it will go well with the food we are serving. Apart from these two points, other factors which affect the decision revolve mainly around what the Lyonnais are prepared to drink. An extraordinary number of them claim that they cannot drink Beaujolais because it is too acid, belying an old joke about the three rivers flowing into Lyon. (The three are, of course, the Saône, the Rhône and wine from the Beaujolais.) In point of fact, the Beaujolais river flows into Paris, where practically nothing else is drunk. The Lyonnais believe that Parisians deserve such thin, meagre, acid stuff, since they do not know any better. After Beaujolais, they claim, a glass of Côtes du Rhône tastes almost like port. My own feeling about this comparison is that Beaujolais is altogether a less serious wine. No 'great' wine comes out of the region, whereas such wines as Côte Rôtie and Châteauneuf du Pape are far more interesting, complex products. As for the bad reputation that Beaujolais has in the Lyonnais area, I think that it is partly the light-hearted character of the wine that is to blame, especially if it is drunk chilled. People tend to quaff it as though it were a sort of fruity drink, forgetting that it is often around 13 per cent alcohol. Small wonder, then, that they feel less well after an evening spent drinking Beaujolais than after an evening of more moderate consumption of Côtes du Rhône.

Heading south from Lyon is always exciting. The 'Autoroute du Soleil' follows the route of the old Nationale 7, immortalized by the French singer Charles Trenet in one of his songs. If you have not heard this work, then I can tell you that it is almost impossible when you are driving down the motorway to stop repeating the refrain to yourself, a very insistent *'Nationale sept, Nationale sept, Nationale sept. . .'*. After a while you begin to regret ever having heard the song. The motorway plunges directly south, down the

Rhône valley, out of Lyon through the industrial area of Feyzin, where there is a line of oil refineries, then on towards the Mediterranean. About an hour and a half from Lyon, the climate suddenly changes and what might have seemed like the frozen north transforms magically into the temperate south. At certain times of year this change can be quite sensational. I have left Lyon with snow falling and, between Valence and Orange, picnicked in the open air in warm sunlight. Of course, experiences like this are not common in December, January or February, since the inland climate of Provence can be very savage. While the Mediterranean coast is certainly mild throughout the winter – indeed, far nicer than when the entire French nation descends on it in June, July and above all August – inland, round the Dentelle de Montmirail, the Montagne du Luberon and the Mont du Ventoux, their peaks rising to almost 2000 metres, with a good strong mistral blowing, the climate can be very harsh. Even so, a coolish spring can turn easily into warm summer, and autumn can be pushed a couple of months further along the calendar, simply by travelling 200 kilometres down the Autoroute du Soleil. '*Vous êtes en Provence*' announces a panel by the side of the motorway, and it carries roughly the weight of notices indicating passage into another country.

Just to the south of Lyon the Rhône valley broadens out and is not particularly inspiring. The river itself is a great wide tract of water without much gaiety about it. It is still considerably navigated by heavy barges. At Valence, an hour and fifteen minutes' drive from Lyon, you are already in Provence. The mountains start to close in again, the quality of light changes and intensifies, and the countryside of rolling hills, punctuated with sharp rocky peaks, begins to look gloriously foreign. Provence truly is another land. The valley produces a vast quantity of wine, so the amount of land given over to vineyards is hardly surprising, but there are also olive groves, with their beautiful grey-green foliage, as well as fruit production of all sorts. Set in this variegated silver, green and golden landscape are long, low, Provençal farmhouses, their shutters closed against the light and heat, surrounded by trees to give shade, their walls bleached almost white by centuries of sunlight. From these southern regions of the Rhône come solid, strong wines made principally with Grenache and Syrah grape varieties. The villages of Vacqueyras, Gigondas (from the Latin *jocunditas*, meaning 'happiness', for obvious reasons), Rasteau and Beaumes-de-Venise all produce lovely wines, dark purple in colour, often between 13 and 14 per cent alcohol, full of Provençal sunlight. We purchase Vacqueyras from Albert Bernard, whose estate, La Garrigue, is actually at Beaumes-de-Venise. It is a beautiful stone house where his family has been producing wine for over 150 years. He also makes a first class Gigondas, but I cannot buy this for the restaurant, since it requires laying down for some years, and if you are selling wine for 70 or 80 francs a bottle, you cannot keep large quantities of it lying in your cellar for years.

Going to choose wine always feels like going on holiday, even though it is part of our job. True, the sort of holiday it provides is very short; generally just a day, even half a day. A trip to the Beaujolais and back can take less than two hours if I am just collecting an order. Of course, I can have the wine delivered – it generally costs an extra 2 francs a bottle – but it is so nice to go and fetch it. Sometimes we can leave on Sunday evening after the restaurant has shut, drive south for three hours, stay the night in a country hotel, spend the next day going around producers, and return home on Monday evening, if necessary stopping off another night on the way. As I approach Lyon, just after the Feyzin refineries, with 'Nationale sept, Nationale sept, Nationale sept' ringing through my head, the motorway swoops over a bridge across the Rhône, very wide at this point since it has just been joined by the Saône, and the idiotic song is knocked from my head by the wonderful view of the city spread out before me. The road is elevated enough to make it possible to see 5 kilometres upstream, beyond the Perrache railway bridge, with long orange TGVs trundling slowly across, to where the Croix Rousse sits in cubist splendour, and to Fourvière, where the elephant casually waves its legs in the air and the mock-Eiffel tower stands. Even the ugly (to my eyes) pencil-shaped tower of the Credit Lyonnais, which dominates the left bank of the Rhône, makes me pleased that I have arrived home.

9

Many people dream of owning a small business. Indeed, many people dream of owning a restaurant, or at least a café or tea-shop. I was astonished at how often, during the period when construction work was going on, I met people who, having asked me what I did in life, claimed that they also had always wanted to run a restaurant. They would then embark on a description of what these restaurants would have been like, and no doubt many of them would have been very nice, though the world has managed to rub along pretty well without them. On the whole, restaurants come into being as the result of an initiative on the part of the owners, rather than to fill an obvious gap in the market. My feeling is that a lot of people think that running a restaurant is similar to inviting a few friends to dinner and spending a pleasant evening with them. There is undoubtedly an element of truth in this image, albeit a small element. It is always nice when friends turn up at the restaurant, especially if it is not too full and you can sit down and talk with them. On the whole, however, when friends are invited to your house, you choose whom you wish to come. You also choose at what time you want them to come and, still more important, what you want them to eat. You can even influence what they wear to your house – 'Don't bother to dress up.' Clearly a restaurant is not like this. Your customers may all wish to eat different things, or, possibly worse, they may all wish to eat the same thing, in which case, unless you operate a freezer-based establishment, you will probably run out of certain dishes. I am constantly asked how I know how much to make of each item on the menu, and the only answer is an annoying 'experience'. On the other hand, I think that it is better to run out of dishes than to have inexhaustible stocks of doubtful freshness in fridges or freezers.

Then there are the running costs. Even if the restaurant is small, and you are running it on your own with a partner or a loved one (may they remain so for ever, even when table one has sent back its third bottle of wine, table two is persistently claiming a jug of water that has been forgotten, and the temperature in the kitchen is physically and emotionally at boiling point), even if there are no salaries involved, and therefore no immediate drain on the till, restaurants are very expensive toys indeed. It is quite possible for a small one to lose money at the rate of about £500 a week if it is operating incorrectly. Three months can see you over £6000 in debt, and suppliers are not likely to offer very much credit to a newly established business. There is a similarity between the joke statistic about motor-cycle accidents – that 60 per cent of them occur within a hundred yards of the showroom – and the percentage of restaurants that go bust within the first three months of opening.

While it would not be true to say that we had given no thought to how we were going to meet the running costs of the restaurant, we had certainly not given it much. My scepticism for the figures which the accountant had produced for us was in no way a reflection of my feelings about him, or about his profession. It was entirely due to the fact that his predictions were based on figures that I had invented, or at the best, calculated myself, so I had a fair idea how far they diverged from the truth. At all events, when we first opened, I believed that it was necessary for us to be open every night of the week except Monday, and at lunchtimes on Wednesday, Thursday and Friday. On Saturday and Sunday we served brunch, or a large English breakfast. For two people, with no assistance at all, to undertake as much work as this was a little over-optimistic, especially considering that those people had, in one case, only a very little professional experience, and in the other case, no experience at all. However, the accountant had informed us that in order to clear 1000 francs a week profit (our joint wages), it was necessary for the restaurant to turn over at 15,000 francs a week. In fact, the restaurant only once exceeded this figure in its first two years of operation – in its eighth week, I think, when we took 18,000 francs. By that time, of course, we were far too exhausted to feel we had done particularly well. Still, we worked away, thinking that bankruptcy was edging nearer and nearer with every passing week. The sum of 15,000 francs a week began to resemble the north face of the Eiger, and we felt like a couple of very inexperienced and ill-equipped mountaineers, with bankruptcy a terrible gaping ravine beneath us. The fact that quite a large sum of money was building up in our account did little to reassure us; I was not even sure that it was really ours, thinking that at any moment it might be confiscated in extra interest rates, or seized by the state as social security payments.

Our days would take the following form. I would get down into the restaurant at around half-past eight in the morning and start preparations for the lunchtime service. We produced three-course lunches at 48 francs. These might consist of a range of pies – a different one each day – a roast stuffed joint, chicken casserole, or even Cornish pasties; a choice of salads or soup as starters, then cheese or dessert to follow. There would be two starters, very occasionally three, and a choice of two main courses, with an attempt at a meat/fish, or a dark meat/light meat or poultry contrast. Sue came down at about half-past nine with Xavier, then aged one. His strong-mindedness and intrepid spirit precluded his staying in a play-pen (he howled solidly if we attempted to keep him in one). Consequently, he was allowed to roam free about the restaurant, playing with the table settings, particularly the knives. Sue would then go to market to buy the lettuce, bread, fish and other produce necessary for the day. It was a curious business, but while at eleven o'clock I would feel that I was well under way, could in fact afford to slow down my preparations, the time between quarter-past eleven and twelve o'clock would mysteriously telescope into itself and it was always a frantic rush at the last minute. It must also be said that the French often like to lunch early. Sometimes as early as half-past eleven, outraged faces would appear at the door (always locked until the official opening hour). If these customers were allowed in to sit down, they would start calling for aperitifs, wine, bread or water, thereby monopolizing a pair of hands indispensable to the final preparations in the kitchen. Now, no doubt we could cope. Then we could not. Finally, just before opening, I had to take Xavier across the road to M. and Mme Dodet, who looked after him during our lunchtime service.

Just as some people would turn up to lunch before opening time, so we would invariably get someone walking in three minutes after the end of service (two o'clock, in our case). This would be somebody who, since they were beginning their lunch so late, could afford to sit around until four o'clock. The worst thing is, of course, to have no one at all for most of the time and then to have two customers arrive at the end of service, who sit there for two hours chatting, but drinking no wine or aperitifs, thus reducing their bill to a minimum. But when you are half-way up the north face of the Eiger, with the awful ravine below you, you have to use every crampon you've got, even if it is only a tiny, bent crampon. Every restaurateur faced with non-spending customers is bound to feel waves of exasperation from time to time. Sometimes it seems as if all the tight-fisted customers in town have singled out your restaurant as the ideal place for them to come specifically *not* to eat what you have laboriously prepared in order for *them* to have a good time, and in order for *you* to make money. On the other hand, there are good lunches or evenings when everybody seems to have come to the restaurant to celebrate, and they make up for the poor days.

Even on days when the lunch service ended at half-past two, there would be at least an hour's clearing up to do before preparation for the evening could begin. Our evening dishes were different from our rather more humble lunch-time dishes, but the same desserts were on offer. Thus all the desserts used up at lunchtime needed to be replaced, and fresh starters and main courses prepared. Sue would try to do her cooking as quickly as possible, then go and fetch Xavier and have as much of the afternoon free as she could. In general, we tried to complete most of the evening preparation before lunch, so that I also could have time off in the afternoon. This was not always possible, and I would often only have time to rush upstairs for a shower at the end of the afternoon, then rush straight back down to finish off the *mise en place* and re-open for the evening service. Some-times, though, I could arrive down in the restaurant at about six o'clock after a relatively relaxed afternoon, make last-minute adjustments to the tables, put the finishing touches to any food that was not completed, and set in motion the cooking of things which were supposed to be ready at eight o'clock. One of the least agreeable surprises that running a restaurant can hold is the realization at half-past seven that the roast which you have been advertising on your door all day has not actually been put in the oven, and has no chance whatsoever of resembling even slightly a piece of cooked meat by eight o'clock, especially if the roast in question is a rolled shoulder of pork, stuffed with apples, prunes and sage, which needs a good two hours' cooking.

At seven we try to eat, sitting at a table towards the back of the restaurant with Xavier. Originally we ate after the service, but that meant going to bed very late, so now we are more professional about it, and eat before. The main disadvantage of eating before the doors open is that we are likely to be interrupted by the phone ringing, or by people coming and pushing at the door, kept locked until eight o'clock. Sometimes these are people who want to reserve for later on; sometimes they are people who want to eat straight away and who can't believe that the restaurant should only open at eight. Occasionally they suggest that they can come in and have a drink while they wait, and occasionally this is all right. However, if it is only ten past seven, then the wait is going to be a long one, and besides, we are trying to have a quiet meal before the rush. Worse still are those who stop only to apply for information – 'I had some delicious lamb with mint sauce in England; how do you make mint sauce?' – while our supper is going cold. The problem is that the restaurant is a public place, and when the public finds itself shut out, then it doesn't always understand. The public may also, arriving in front of our restaurant, which has big windows without curtains, mistake us for customers eating. This provokes outraged shovings at the door, followed by inquiring looks and then loud tappings. Few things are more disturbing to people trying to have a quiet meal than these inquiring looks and loud tappings.

Our meals almost always end in a rush. The table must be cleared and reset, and the door opened for the first people reserved, who will almost always manage to arrive five minutes early. Xavier must be put to bed and have a story read to him by Sue, and I must start off on the round of welcoming customers, taking coats, showing people to their tables, taking orders for aperitifs and so on. As the restaurant is small, we tend to work a fair amount with reservations. In general, even if all the reservations are for eight o'clock or half-past eight, people will not all arrive at once; it's nice if they arrive at roughly ten-minute intervals. We take our last orders at around half-past ten, though we can be persuaded to hang on a bit longer, if people reserve for a meal after a show. We have ten tables and a maximum capacity, limited by the number of chairs we possess, of thirty customers. We don't turn tables very often, but on a busy night, we might do an extra three tables, with a maximum of perhaps forty covers. Frankly, we don't have the food for any more. On the other hand, we do sometimes refuse quite a lot of people – either by telephone or at the door, and although this is obviously a good thing, since it shows the restaurant is working, it is unfortunate to have to turn people away. I suppose that it sometimes makes people want to come more, but on other occasions they must say to themselves that there is no point in trying Higgins, since it is always full. Unfortunately, this is by no means the case. If only they would try on a typically intimate Wednesday evening, involving just us and two customers.

The Lyonnais are rather casual about reserving seats in a restaurant; there is such a huge choice anyway, that if one is full, there will always be room elsewhere. Often people will telephone to ask whether we are open on such and such a night: 'Is it necessary to reserve?' they ask, having already indicated that they intend to come. Even though they are on the telephone, they do not want to ask for a table to be kept for them. I find this a difficult question to deal with in my persona as patron, proud of his business. To say 'No, of course not, there is always loads of space in my restaurant,' is tantamount to admitting that my restaurant is not really very good. I have also run up against the problem of not insisting that people reserve, and then being obliged to refuse them at the door of a fully booked restaurant. This makes them furious: 'We rang you and asked,' they say indignantly. And I can understand their fury: our restaurant is out of the way, so people who come to it have almost always made a special detour to get here. On the other hand, there have been many occasions when I have strictly stipu-lated to people that they must reserve, sometimes stopping them just before they hang up and telling them how impor-tant it is, only to be standing in a totally empty restaurant when they arrive, and in consequence having to suffer super-cilious smiles.

Solutions to these and other problems appeared no clearer as we approached the end of the first year of Higgins. Trade went up and down. The singer David Bowie came to perform in Lyon and for a while we became obsessed with the idea of luring him to the restaurant as a sure way of filling the place up, the publicity value of one David Bowie being quite unmeasurable on the Richter scale. The question was how to get him to come. We discussed this at some length, our ideas becoming more and more far-fetched. The ultimate suggestion was Sue's: 'We could write to him,' she said 'and say something like this: "Dear David, you may be interested to know that even in these days of spiralling prices, in our restaurant you can buy a half bottle of Côtes du Rhône for 27 francs"'. We then collapsed with laughter at the idea of a multi-millionaire pop star being attracted to the place because of the reasonableness of its half bottles of wine. We didn't write the letter, and Bowie didn't come.

The weather turned ferociously cold, and thick fogs squeezed along the narrow Croix-Rousse streets, scarcely dissipated by the pale midday sun. I rewarded such customers as we had for their bravery in coming out in such weather with nips of whisky on arrival, and cursed our extremely expensive heating system, which was proving hopelessly inadequate for dealing with temperatures dropping to minus 15 degrees centigrade. We bought more electric radiators and left the oven doors open. Sometimes I would amuse myself by going and looking at the madly whirring electricity meter. The very cumbersome books which our first accountant insisted we keep were handed over to him for his annual audit, and we waited with bated breath to see whether we were going to survive into a second year.

'*Le resultat*', he announced, '*n'est pas magnifique.*' In our first year's trading, it turned out that the total profit of the restaurant had been 1539 francs. This meant that our wages had been roughly £3 a week, or £1.50 each. So how had we lived on £1.50 a week each? Well, we hadn't. We had lived on money that I had earned translating a book called *The Arts of the Twenties*, which I undertook just as the restaurant opened, and we lived on the VAT credit we had accumulated from the alterations we had carried out. It must be admitted that this was not a promising beginning, but we did not really stop to think. We were still in the honeymoon period with our new restaurant. We had started to find the rhythm of the job, trade was looking up, and besides, tomorrow would always be another day.

I suppose that our first year was spent coming to terms with having our own business – facing up to the demands that it made on us and trying to organize our lives in such a way that we were not overwhelmed. Restaurants are notoriously hard work. Basically, Sue and I divide the labour quite simply: I am the waiter and she is the cook. At least, this is how the customers see us. Until relatively recently the majority of small or medium sized restaurants would be run the other way round, with the man in the kitchen and the woman in the room. I confess that it sometimes occurs to me that trade would benefit if Sue, who is very pretty, and who now speaks French with just the right degree of English accent, could be persuaded to go out into the room and teeter round in high heels and tight skirts. But what kind of a job is that for a man's wife? On the occasions when she did sally out into the room, in the early days when she didn't speak good French, some fairly interesting misunderstandings resulted: '*Ce sont des oeufs à plat*' she announced at one brunch table, instead of '*oeufs au plat*', suggesting that the eggs had been punctured and deflated like a burst tyre. Even more gloriously, '*Je cuis le foie de veau à poil*' was delivered to another table of interested men, keen to witness this interesting technique combining cooking and nudity (she meant '*à la poêle*', in a frying-pan). At all events Sue claims that she does not much care for the customers and is too shy to want to talk to them, whereas I positively enjoy meeting them; well, most of the time. In reality a lot of the cooking is done by me – all pastry, all puddings and all terrines – while Sue does most main dishes and all Indian dishes.

The relationship between the kitchen and the dining room is curiously disjointed, since all the cook knows about the customers is what they are eating and what the waiter has said about them. It is thus possible for me to pop into the kitchen, make some faintly disparaging remark about a certain table, go back out into the dining room, and then return to the kitchen to find Sue consumed with rage about that particular table, simply because the only information she had about it was bad. I am then obliged to calm her down and stop her from 'going straight out and giving them a piece of my mind – that would show them!'; as she doesn't mince her words, it probably would show them very clearly indeed. But in the meantime I may have discovered that my first impression was entirely wrong and that they were in fact thoroughly pleasant people.

The truth is that when we first opened, we felt hopelessly amateur. To an extent even, we felt that we were frauds and not real restaurateurs: Sue was a doctor and I was a translator, and we were just playing at owning a restaurant. One small thing which reinforced this feeling of amateurishness at the beginning was our costume. It may be the case that the cowl doesn't make the monk, but it certainly helps. Initially we wore T-shirts and plastic aprons in the kitchen. T-shirts are unsuitable since they leave too much of the arms bare and prone to burning by spitting fat or other sources of airborne heat. Plastic aprons are unsuitable because you cannot wipe your hands on them and because they melt when they come into contact with the hot stove. Also they are absurd garments, and they tend to have coyly amusing slogans like 'Hello, I'm Mister Cheese' printed on them, or advertising for products like Bovril or drinking chocolate, and why anyone should willingly transform themselves into a walking advertisement is beyond me. To wear ordinary clothes while cooking in a professional kitchen is a bad idea, since they very quickly adopt the smells of the food, especially if the food is spicy, and nobody wants to go around smelling like a tandoori chicken. So, after a few months of the restaurant, we ordered long white linen aprons and white chefs' jackets with 'Mister Higgins' embroidered on them in blue and red, and cooks' checked trousers. Sue and I are sufficiently similar in size for us to be able to order the same size garments. After all, these were working clothes, not our entry for a *concours d'élégance*. Sue would look charmingly waifish in her slightly large outfit, and I, so I imagined, would look dashingly powerful in my slightly small outfit, the buttons straining a little across my chest. The clothes were delivered by parcel post, and when they finally arrived, we were very excited and rushed upstairs to try them on. Two minutes later, one charmingly waifish cook and one dashingly powerful cook looked at themselves in the mirror in their flat, and felt for the first time like the professional owners of a real restaurant.

10

Which is the most important part of an aeroplane: the wings, the fuselage, or the motor? It's an interesting question, with a philosophical slant. An aeroplane with no wings will not fly. But then, nor will an aeroplane with no fuselage, since there will be nowhere for the pilot to sit, so if the machine did get off the ground, it would almost certainly crash. Of course, if it had no motor, it simply wouldn't move at all. The answer is that all three elements are necessary. As far as Mr Higgins was concerned, we had two of the elements, with the restaurant itself as wings and fuselage, and us as pilots. The role of the motor can perhaps be given to the customers. Two questions are clearly of primary interest to the owners of a new restaurant: how to get customers to come, and how to deal with them when they are there.

We had been warned that the Lyonnais were cold and reserved and liked to keep themselves to themselves, and I think it's true that they are a cliquey lot with a definite tendency to stick together and mistrust anyone coming from beyond the boundaries of the Lyon conglomeration. Even the Viennois, from 20 kilometres away, are viewed with suspicion, while the Stéphanois, from Saint-Etienne (all of 47 kilometres away), might as well be green with long tentacles and a purple tube for a nose. When a Lyonnais opens a restaurant, he has a guaranteed clientele made up of his school friends, his university or college friends, and above all, his family. And my God, their families are big! Endless ramifications of different degrees and removes of cousinship fill innumerable Lyonnais restaurants. Of course, the blood-bond is not enough to shore up a place which is bad, but it helps enormously for a while. On the other hand, while the Lyonnais are wary of other French tribes – especially the Parisian tribe – I think that we, being British, fell outside the boundaries of such visceral suspicion. Thus the Lyonnais bourgeoisie – families whose grandparents and great-grandparents have come from Lyon – have occasionally deigned to visit the restaurant. If it were a restaurant *tenu par des Parisiens*, they wouldn't even cross the threshold – or not for at least ten years.

What we had initially – what we still have, indeed – was curiosity value. We were the only English restaurant in Lyon, possibly the only English restaurant proper in France, the others being teashops or pubs which also serve meals. Moreover, we were in Lyon, and therefore firmly within the seventh circle of gastronomic heaven. Consequently, quite soon we started to attract a kind of 'freak-show' clientele, though not in an altogether negative sense – everybody is entitled to feel curiosity of a non-morbid sort over oddities – and it is quite a tribute to the population of this city that so many of them were adventurous enough to try out a cuisine that they have been brought up to consider appalling. It is still more of a tribute that a fair percentage was willing to revise its opinion at the end of the meal, and concede that the British way of cooking had something to offer.

Advertising in general is too expensive in France, perhaps in Britain also, for restaurants like ours to indulge in much. Consequently, we relied almost exclusively on word of mouth, depending on friends to spread the good news. After the restaurant had been open for some weeks, however, we were visited by a talkative man with glasses and a briefcase. He told us he was a journalist on a local newspaper called *Croix-Rousse Actualité*, and that he very much appreciated our restaurant and would like to write an article about it. How pleased we were! He visited us several times and asked a lot of questions. Finally the article was ready and presented to us for our approval. It was certainly very complimentary, if a little short. Did we find it satisfactory? We thought it lovely. In that case, it was 1500 francs plus VAT. I protested that I had thought the article was free. The article, yes, we were told, but not the advertisement that went with it, and without which the article would not appear. What we were encountering here was the phenomenon of *publiredactionelle*: a free article written on the purchase of an advertisement. On this occasion, we took the article, but I must say that I felt absurdly innocent, and very much as though I had been tricked. It turned out to be useless advertising anyway, and I suspect that it even had a negative effect – we had fewer customers than if we had not taken it. This formed my totally biased approach to *Croix-Rousse Actualité* which is now to boycott all establishments which take its advertising.

At the beginning, then, it was simple curiosity that brought most people to the restaurant. But we did have other attractions. Right from the start we began to get groups of language students or school children. On several occasions, the whole place was filled at lunchtime with giggling 13-year-olds being encouraged by their teachers to sing English songs. Sometimes these visits were agreeable, sometimes not. Eventually I stopped taking school children, since it was such hard work and so unprofitable – teachers would try to negotiate the lowest price possible, as children could not be expected to pay much. Once a teacher turned up with insufficient money to pay, forcing me to accept 5 francs less per pupil. Then, of course, they would drink no wine or aperitifs – not that I would have wanted hordes of drunken adolescents regularly to be seen emerging from the restaurant. But, more to the point, a restaurateur who was trying to gain serious acceptance did not want to transform himself into an extension of the French scholastic system.

On the other hand, we continue to receive groups of students from language schools, and I have come to know quite a number of the language teachers themselves, who come back regularly with the same or different students. In the month of June, just before the long summer holidays, we have a group almost every night, sometimes two. Mostly these groups come and go in a rather faceless way, sometimes calling out 'See you next year' as they leave. Though meant kindly, this always upsets me, since it implies that they wouldn't consider coming to the restaurant out of the context of their group. Sometimes I am requested to speak English to these groups, which is all right if they have a level above the absolutely rudimentary, but quite impossible if they don't. Very often I detect that they are people who have no chance whatsoever of learning English, least of all by coming to an English restaurant in the hope of picking the language up by osmosis. Very often they are bored, or shy, and go to the classes primarily for the social life. Sometimes, however, a particular character stands out. This was the case in a group of students of the *'troisième age'*, OAPs who came to lunch on two occasions. All these people spoke excellent English, and presumably went to the classes to keep their brains alert, and to avoid forgetting the language. One of the first to arrive was an extremely elegant woman of about seventy.

'Good morning,' she announced brightly, coming straight forward to shake my hand. 'Are you the owner? How are you?'

'I'm fine, thank you. How are you?'

'I'm full of beans!'

'Yes,' I replied, avoiding comment on this 1930s slang. 'Would you like a drink while you're waiting for the others?'

'Yes, of course, a little snifter – perhaps a couple of fingers of whisky.' Where, I wondered, did one have to learn English to find out about 'fingers' of whisky? But she *was* absolutely full of beans. She came back the following year and she was still as beanish as ever, and although I haven't seen her since, I shouldn't think that the beans have diminished too much.

Other people come to the restaurant through simple affection for Britain: those who have visited the country as tourists, or to learn the language, and have come away with pleasant memories of the place – after all, it's a lovely country. I remember a man telling me once that on the last occasion he had been in Britain he had been unable to get any bread: he had been with the Free French under De Gaulle during World War II, and bread had been unobtainable. Despite this terrible lack (for a Frenchman), he clearly had a deep affection for the British. Some of those who have visited England in recent years may even have been lucky and eaten quite well in country or city pubs, or at restaurants carrying on the revival of English cuisine inspired in the 1980s by chefs like Michael Smith and John Tovey. But think of the food that was on offer in many hotels in the 1970s, particularly the starters: soup of the day, brown or red and directly out of a tin, or a choice of orange or tomato juice, described as 'fresh' but also coming from a tin. What did they think they were playing at? Imagine if I had opened a restaurant serving meals like that, with a grey roast as the main course, served with Brussels sprouts and boiled *and* horrid soft roast potatoes. It's scarcely surprising that the French came back with such a negative picture of Britain's cooking.

Most of all our clientele is made up of people like us. This is quite logical: since we have designed a restaurant in which we feel comfortable, it is natural that it should appeal to people with similar tastes. Thus we tend to have large numbers of young professionals: doctors, dentists, lawyers, a fair number of architects and quite a lot of ad-men. Then there are the artists: painters – whose work we exhibit, providing we like it – actors, dancers, writers and musicians all come as well, especially for Sunday brunch, when the relaxed, rather smoky atmosphere seems to suit them.

On the whole, our customers are a nice lot, and I have come to know many of them quite well over the years. Some, of course, become real friends. I suppose that the fact of a French person coming to an English restaurant already bears witness to a sympathetic openness of mind. Sometimes when I am in other people's restaurants, I look around at the customers and thank heaven that they don't come to my place. However, in Higgins, the 'comedy of manners' element sometimes takes a more farcical turn, and while I have never had wives or husbands turning up to surprise their partners eating tête-à-tête with a third party, I have had husbands and wives turning up individually with illicit partners, which, in a small city, seems to me to be rash behaviour. One such couple we came to refer to as '*deux plats suffisants*' ('two courses only'). These two were aged about fifty; the wife quite good looking, but very severe, the husband subdued and a little plump. '*Deux plats suffisent chez vous*' the wife would announce in a stern way as they sat down; '*nous ne prendrons donc pas de dessert.*' Then, looking very strictly at the husband, on whom a cloud of despondency seemed to be gathering, '*Nous boirons de l'eau.*' No dessert, no wine – The cloud of despondency engulfed the waiter as well.

One day, the wife turned up with a boyfriend. This poor man was rather thin and was in the process of losing his defenceless-looking fluffy blond hair – restaurateurs are very sensitive to the tops of people's heads – but he was a good ten years younger than she. The scenario was identical. But some minutes after I had delivered a jug of water to the table, the man called me back, and in a blustery, nervous way, delivered himself of his last vestiges of independence by announcing, while avoiding his partner's eye, that he would *'quand-même prendre un de vos cocktails'*. When, some moments afterwards, the woman got up to go to the loo, I wanted to go across and tell him about her, whispering in his ear: 'I've seen her often, you know, *and* her husband – you wouldn't want to end up like him. I really think you should go. Now – immediately; she probably won't even notice – '. Later that week, the husband turned up with a girlfriend, at least twenty years younger than he. Cocktails were ordered on the way to the table, followed by two more – one and a half bottles of wine, two desserts and then brandy. There was much hilarity, and it was clear that he had been longing to behave like this for a long time.

One thing that we have learned over the years is that nothing fills the restaurant so quickly as a good newspaper review. We had our first review within a few weeks of opening the restaurant and since then have had a fair number. Journalists probably find it easier to write about an English restaurant than about yet another French restaurant, where the difference between one *andouillette à la moutarde* and another must be infinitely difficult to calculate; the food that the critic eats in our restaurant is almost certainly something he has never eaten before, so he can judge it purely on its own merits. Our first article was written by Pierre Grison, who is the most prolific restaurant reviewer in Lyon, officially based at the Lyon paper *Le Progrès*, but actually stringing for at least six other periodicals. He introduced himself at the end of the meal, saying he had enjoyed it very much and was going to write a notice about us. For a while we went around basking in the light of critical acclaim – surely everyone had read the highly favourable article in *Le Progrès*? Well, not everybody is quite so interested in restaurant reviews as restaurateurs, but we certainly felt the effect of the article for a couple of weeks after its publication.

On the other hand, we have also had three less favourable articles, and these are terrible. On the whole I think the authors had come to the restaurant with a preconceived idea of what they thought it should be like: when it failed to correspond to this image, instead of trying to understand what we were doing, they attacked. One of these articles was not exactly unfavourable, I suppose, but the woman who wrote it took, excusably, since taste is a subjective matter, against the décor of the restaurant, which I think of as 'restrained', but which some find cold. Less excusably, and in my view utterly incomprehensibly, she took against me. The article was about brunch. Having written a few lines praising the scones, the cake, the marmalade, all made with loving care, she claimed, by Sue (despite her being well aware that they were made by me), she ended the article with the words: '*Le décor, hélàs, est en parfait accord avec l'acceuil du patron: glacial.'* ('The décor, alas, perfectly matches the patron's welcome: chilly.')

This article appeared in the colour supplement of the Saturday edition of *Le Figaro* and, despite measuring only three inches square and being hidden on page 14726 of the paper, was found and read by hundreds of people. I was astonished at the power of the press. One customer actually said to me afterwards, *'Vous savez, vous avez mauvaise réputation à Lyon – on vous dit très froid –'* 'You've been reading the Figaro,' I said. But no, she never read the *Figaro*, or perhaps, yes, the other day in the doctor's waiting room. An article written by one woman had thus been transformed into a collective opinion: a reputation. Even if the remarks made by the customers were kind, the article seemed somehow to have become part of their unconscious knowledge: *'Comment ça se fait'*, one woman asked nicely, *'qu'on vous dit glacial, alors que vous êtes si charmant?'* It might just have been a lack of thought on her part, but she said 'You are said to be frosty', rather than 'I have read – '. However, this article was not too bad on the whole, and it did in fact bring us quite a lot of customers. The other two poor reviews we have had were both written by the same man, and he, quite simply, seems to have decided to hate us.

The principal problem appears to be that he absolutely adores Ireland, and our restaurant, despite a degree of Irishness on my side, is not sufficiently Irish. Why is there no Irish stew on the menu? No colcannon? None of the other marvels of the Emerald Isle's cuisine? His last article seemed to me to be terribly unfair, since it began: *'Dans un éspace à trois quarts vide* – but he had come to the restaurant on an awful, rainy Wednesday night, and frankly, if he had wanted to find a full restaurant that night, then the place to look would have been McDonald's in the city centre. In a town like Lyon, no matter how good your restaurant is, to fill it every night is just about impossible. When we went to Paul Bocuse's restaurant at Collanges, it was not even a quarter full. In one of the best restaurants I know in Lyon – Chez Jean Fan-Fan, where the menus cost between 90 and 160 francs, and the cooking is superb – I have rarely seen more than half the seats occupied, and there are only twenty-five of them. Still, we have something to be thankful for: this critic's last article was sufficiently nasty for him never to attempt to come to the restaurant again.

The question of how to treat your customers once they start to come to the restaurant is also important – how to maximize the chances of their coming back, or becoming regulars. Ours is typical of many small restaurants in France in that it is very personal. French people attach great importance to the way they are greeted – the *acceuil*. The British are rather different in this respect, being by and large quite content to slip unnoticed into a restaurant, indeed even prepared to find their own seats if need be. The British, if one can generalize, like to be ignored in shops and restaurants; the French like to be noticed. The warmth of the *acceuil* is definitely part of the profession in France, and while restaurateurs may not go as far as the Americans in calling out 'Missing you already' to departing customers, they are certainly in there wishing customers a nice day with the *bonne journée* formula.

My relationship with my customers is relaxed, and so is my style of service. I am aware of the rule about serving from the right and removing plates from the left – or it may be the other way round – but I cannot for the life of me see the point of it. Nor is it always possible in my restaurant, where there simply isn't room for the server to circulate all round the tables. We don't produce the sort of food that inspires reverent silence or provokes 'gasps of wonder' or 'cries of surprise' as it is put down on the table. Our food is relatively uncomplicated, made daily with thoroughly fresh ingredients. People say that it looks nice as I serve it, but its undoubted niceness is of the appetizing sort rather than the artistic sort. Being a friendly person, I am inclined to talk to my customers, provided they appear to want to talk to me. And, in general, they do want to talk. Many people seem to be genuinely interested in why a couple of British people should ever have come to open an English restaurant in Lyon. Then again, in France there is a definite tradition of the loquacious '*patron*', who is allowed to state his point of view in a way that would have been considered extraordinary in Britain until a few years ago – at least outside a pub, where landlords have always been expected to speak their minds.

In France, customers treat the waiter with a great deal more respect than the British do. Perhaps this is changing in England now, but I have often felt the British do not exactly understand whether the waiter is a human being to be spoken to, or a sort of servant, who should be ignored. As a waiter, I incline to the former point of view. Not so very long ago in a relatively fashionable restaurant in London, I remember being served very well by a Sicilian. The food was not especially good, but the service was excellent and joyous. Next to us, and far too close from my point of view – the law of economics having dictated to the owner that it was necessary to cram as many tables in as possible – was a table for four who, when they were not being imperious with the waiter ('Bring me another bottle of your best plonk, my man'), were making fun of him for not being British, for not speaking English well, and possibly for being homosexual. None of these things concerned them in the least, but they were unable to prevent themselves making bibulous comment on them at the waiter's expense. This would be very unlikely to happen in France. I can honestly say that in eight years of running the restaurant, I doubt if I have had more than ten customers who have been rude to me, and now that I come to think of it, two of those have been British.

But even if I was not a garrulous type, I would have been obliged to speak to the customers since, for the first couple of years of the restaurant, the menu was written in English, without a word of French on it. This meant that I had to do a translation at each table, before the customers could be certain what they were going to eat. And the French generally do like to be clear about what is in a dish. They can take exception to a single ingredient and not want to eat the food as a result. Indian dishes, for example, with sauces made from a blend of cardamoms, coriander, cumin, turmeric, fresh ginger, garlic, onion, cinnamon and cloves, not to mention bay and curry leaves, paprika and chillies, may be unacceptable because of the inclusion of cinnamon – not a spice dear to the French, or at least the Lyonnais, palate. So I would do a tour of the tables and explain our habitual, short menu of five starters and three main courses, as well as explaining the rather unusual house aperitifs. This would of course encourage conversation, and I would be further retained at each table, unable to go on to another, more recently arrived group to give them the menu, and also unable to go back to the kitchen to collect and deliver food that was ready to go out to earlier arrivals. As we got busier, the system became too cumbersome, and the oral tradition was ultimately replaced with a menu that was fully explained in French, leaving room for self expression only in the aperitifs and the desserts.

Ownership of a restaurant can provoke powerful emotions, and one's relationship to the client is not always clear. If you have the sort of restaurant where you welcome your customers as friends and start to know a few details about their private lives – their jobs, their children, their new flat and so on – it is easy to fall into the trap of telling them all sorts of personal problems which will not interest them at all: people go to restaurants to forget that sort of thing, not to wallow in it. Conversely, if working in close contact with a public out to enjoy itself makes you begin to nurture a deep hatred of humankind in general, it is perhaps time to stop working as a restaurateur and take up some less sociable role. A friend of mine who owned a restaurant for a number of years could be heard muttering, shortly before selling the business, that he was frequently tempted to mount a machine-gun on the bar, so he could 'mow them all down as they come in'. Luckily for him and his customers, he did not have time to realize this attractive scheme.

Involvement with one's customers is all a question of degree. My brother has a story about a meal he once had with a friend in a country restaurant in Wiltshire which illustrates the point with considerable force. Throughout the meal, which apparently touched the pinnacles of mediocrity, sounds of increasing clumsiness from the kitchen – smashing of plates and glasses, the ringing of saucepans falling on tiled floors, cutlery sliding down the draining board into the sink – suggested that the chef was drinking heavily. His appearance at the end of the meal confirmed this impression, as he emerged from the kitchen to greet his customers: there were only two, my brother and his friend. It also became clear that his drunkenness was not of the joyous, hilarious sort, but of the woebegone and maudlin type. This cook had been drinking to forget.

'My friends,' he said, helping himself to a glass of their wine, putting his arm round each of their shoulders and slumping heavily forward, 'let me tell you about my divorce . . .'.

11

Cooking for a restaurant full of twenty-five or thirty people, all wanting to eat different things, is a dangerous job, make no mistake about it. The first necessity is a very powerful stove. Ours has two ovens. One of these can be adjusted for keeping things warm; the other can be put on a high temperature for browning dishes or cooking pastry. We also have three open burners on top of the stove, and a couple of biggish hot plates. With all these going at once, it gets very, very warm in the kitchen, so an extremely efficient extraction system is also required. The stove becomes burning hot, and has to be handled with great care – even non-heating elements get hot enough to burn your fingers – and the inside of the ovens becomes lethal. When we first started, our wrists were covered with burns from touching the oven shelves when taking things out of the ovens, and even now we occasionally have an accident when under pressure.

There is a traditional French saying about professional cooking. It's a repetitive little proverb which reflects the repetitiveness of a great deal of the job, with the same things to be done every day. It maintains that the most important thing about restaurant cooking is *'la mise en place, la mise en place, et ensuite, la mise en place'*. 'Mise en place' doesn't simply mean setting tables, but covers all the preparation in the kitchen as well, which, properly done, is the way to stay cool and avoid accidents as far as possible. For example, if a dish is to be served with carrots tossed in butter, mange-tout peas and *gratin dauphinois*, then you must have the par-boiled carrots, and a clean saucepan in which to heat them with the butter ready to hand. The gratin must be keeping warm in the oven, and you must have another saucepan with water simmering in it for the peas. You must also have the dinner plates close to you, to be put in the oven to warm at the last minute – and not to be forgotten about, or the waiter will burn his fingers on them (a classic way for a cook to express his hatred of the serving staff). If you are serving a main course which is fried at the last minute, the pan then having to be deglazed, say with Madeira, and a sauce con-structed with veal stock, mustard and cream – for example for lamb's kidneys – then all these things must be within your reach as well, otherwise you'll be running all over the place, leaving pans too long on the flame, or forgetting to put food into the oven. Of course, if you are a major chef in a big kitchen with a brigade of sous-chefs and apprentices behind you, then you can just call for anything you need, and it will magically appear. If you are on your own, organization is essential.

This main course then has to be assembled on the plate, so you also need a good array of serving spoons to dish everything out with; serving tongs are an indispensable tool in this respect. A restaurant with ten tables may require you to be finishing off one order at the same time as starting another, and each order may be made up of dishes which take quite different times to cook, and have to be planned accordingly. At first it is all quite nightmarish, but you do get used to it. The order must be planned around the parts which take the longest to cook, and these must go into the oven as soon as the starter has left the kitchen. For example, we serve grilled fillets of Finnan haddock with a sauce made from wine, butter, cream, parsley and mace. This sauce can't stand too much reheating, but it can be kept warm on top of the oven, not actually on a direct flame. A fillet of haddock takes only four minutes to cook under the grill, so can be done in the last few moments. If the other part of this order has been tandoori chicken and steak and kidney pie, which take twenty minutes to cook, then these must be done first. If the table has not ordered starters, then it must be warned that all the main courses are cooked to order and may take some time. Our pies are served in individual bowls, and are prepared in the following way: the basic mixture is cooked beforehand and kept in a container in the fridge; the pastry is rolled out and cut into circles the right size for the bowls, and a box of pastry decorations – leaves and flowers – is prepared in advance and lightly floured to stop the bits sticking to each other. When the order comes in, I fill a pie bowl with the mixture, brush a pastry disc with beaten egg (the beaten egg and the brush being *en place* already), apply the decoration, and whack the lot into a hot oven for about fifteen minutes, reducing the heat after about eight minutes. It's a good idea to set a timer for eight minutes here, because if you forget the pie and it burns, then obviously it holds up the whole order twenty minutes. In terms of waiting at a table for food, twenty minutes is acceptable, forty is generally not. The moral is that if you have to make a mistake, make it with a dish that cooks quickly.

In between preparing the main courses, the starters have to be set out. The Lyonnais love salads, but are not keen on soup (considered to be 'peasant food'). We persist in serving soup, which is so popular a starter in Britain, but always have at least two salads in our list of starters. All the elements for these must also be *en place*, set out on a work surface in separate bowls or containers. We try to use a mixture of different sorts of lettuce leaves – red oak-leaf, curly endive, lamb's lettuce and so forth – and this is all washed and dried (as far as possible) before the service and stored in a large plastic bag in the fridge (incidentally the *definitive* way to keep lettuce leaves fresh). Then there is a big, round-bottomed bowl, known rather vulgarly in French as a *cul de poule* ('hen's bottom'), into which the leaves are tossed and dressed. These are arranged on plates, and the various bits that are to go into the salad are arranged artistically on top, sprinkled with chives or parsley, chopped cress or little tomato jewels, and sent off to the table.

All this preparation is necessary to serve a menu which typically looks like this:

Spotted Dick, S'il Vous Plait

Cream of tomato soup with fresh basil

*

Duck terrine cooked in port and served with
cranberry sauce

*

Miniature smoked haddock pies with wild mushrooms

*

Smoked salmon, chicken, avocado and walnut salad,
with walnut oil dressing

*

Marinated mushroom salad in mint, coriander, olive oil
and lemon juice marinade

* — * — *

STEAK AND KIDNEY PIE

*

HALIBUT FISHCAKES STUFFED WITH PRAWNS,
SERVED ON TOMATO SAUCE

*

LAMB ROGAN JOSH

* — * — *

Cheese and dessert

We try to plan the three main courses so that one (a stew) is
bubbled on top of the stove in a saucepan, one is baked in
the oven, and the other is cooked quickly at the last minute,
either by frying or by putting it into a very hot oven, as one
might do for tandoori chicken. The idea of doing Indian
dishes came from Sue, who understands very well how to
balance the mixture of spices, and is able to deal with the
cooking technique which involves frying the concoction of

spices before adding the meat. There are a few Indian restaurants in Lyon – perhaps five – but none of them is especially interesting. We serve our Indian dishes with a selection of chutneys and relishes, but do not normally make the special breads that go with them. Our list of puddings might include lemon cheesecake, chocolate pie, apple and banana crumble, coffee mousse flavoured with Irish whiskey and served with hot chocolate sauce, trifle with peaches and strawberries, and anything else we have time to make. The French love puddings and are, in fact, far more appreciative of them than the British, rightly recognizing that we have understood the essence of what makes a proper dessert. If our list of food sounds rather simple for a restaurant, that's because our policy was that it was better to do something simple well than to attempt something more complicated and not pull it off. At any rate, the formula has proved a success, and while we have become a little more adventurous over the years, we have not changed fundamentally.

Our house aperitif is Bucks Fizz, which we make with fresh orange juice and champagne, as opposed to fizzy white wine. Made like this it is a lovely drink – the French find it unusual, since most restaurants serve kirs, or variations on them – and it appeals to their taste for drinking something slightly sweet before a meal, where a British person might take a glass of white wine. The only problem with Bucks Fizz made in this way is that when the two ingredients are brought together in a champagne flute, they explode in a burst of bubbles on contact – particularly if the bottle of champagne has just been opened, and the orange juice just squeezed. Unless the ingredients are brought together very slowly, adding the orange to the champagne drop by drop at first, then the drink will fizz out over the top of the flute. This means that it takes quite a long time to make a number of the drinks, and this can delay the service.

We also serve a *cocktail du moment* as well as a non-alcoholic cocktail. These are both shaken at the table by the waiter, to the great amusement of the customers. The main reason for this amusement, apart from the fact that it is unusual to have a drink shaken for you at your table, is that the waiter, try as he might, has never been able to cultivate the cool, off-hand shaking of the professional barman, who can even carry on a conversation at the same time as he prepares a drink. The waiter in this case hangs on to the shaker like grim death and gives the beastly thing the shaking of its life, watching it suspiciously all the time, since he has never been entirely able to rid himself of the fear that it may explode. One customer once remarked that it was almost as if the shaker was shaking the waiter and not the other way around. The French love aperitifs – in fact they are more inclined to take aperitifs than they are to drink wine with their meal, and our cocktails – White Ladies, White Leopards, Whisky Sours and so forth – are a much appreciated feature of the restaurant.

As far as our food is concerned, many things which are typically English, like steak and kidney pie or lamb with mint sauce, which are two strong-tasting dishes, appeal to individual customers, but are not at all to the taste of others. But if there is one dish that seems to achieve across-the-board appreciation, and one that has entered into the mythology of the restaurant, it is meatloaf *en croûte*. It still amuses me that we should have had such a success with something called 'meatloaf'. Can you imagine many British people going to a restaurant because it serves meatloaf? I think you would be hard put to find another restaurant in Europe that even serves the dish. Yet here meatloaf has become one of the *spécialités de la maison*. Very often I hear customers saying to friends that they are bringing to the restaurant for the first time: '*Tiens, il y a un truc extraordinaire, vraiment délicieux, le meatloaf. . .*' Often of course, they do not know what the name means, or that to describe a dish called 'meatloaf' as '*très fin*' is more or less a translingual contradiction in terms. Our version of meatloaf, however, is a rather grand one, made with minced pork, layered with cheese and mushrooms and then wrapped up in pastry. It's not a recipe of my own invention, except that I discovered some years ago that the meat mixture should not be at all dry when raw, and that adding a good lot of veal stock or strong Bovril, until it is almost as slack as thick porridge, transforms the dish beyond all recognition. Served with a knob of mustard and parsley butter, a vegetable in sauce, like cauliflower, and another green vegetable for colour, sliced meatloaf can be made to look quite elegant on the plate. Individual slices can be cut in advance and wrapped up separately in very thin pastry parcels, or the meatloaf can be cooked as an entity in its own right, kept warm and sliced as it is needed. It's an easy dish to serve, since it is entirely made in advance, and requires no last-minute adjustments.

You might imagine that the intricate preparation that I

have described, coupled with the relatively simple formula of the restaurant, would mean that everything would always go according to plan. But you would be mistaken. Things can, and do, go gloriously wrong, and to a certain extent the job of the restaurateur can often be thought of as 'how best to get out of a catastrophe'. Another, more philosophical, conception might be to consider the restaurant as the safe 'middle enclosure' in the midst of chaos, as in the ancient Norse vision of the world. The chaos comes bursting in through the door with the customers. We must fight heroically on, but ultimately we are doomed to defeat. In concrete terms, how, for example, to deal with the lunchtime when our meat delivery had still not arrived, although several tables of customers were already in place? Would the best solution be to put on a disguise and stand outside the restaurant warning people not to go in? Or simply to simulate a dead faint in front of the door? How can one explain to a customer who has just chosen three consecutive out-of-stock wines from the list that he is being guided in his choice by malign powers, and that the only way to resist them is to make a specific effort to choose a bottle of wine that he actively does not want? What is to be done when a bowl cracks in a hot oven, spilling boiling fat onto the oven floor, which instantly ignites, sending a sheet of flame out into the kitchen? Is the correct solution to spray the oven and its contents with the fire extinguisher which we keep near the stove, or is it to close the oven door and count to ten, smiling confidently at any customers who may have seen the flames, as though this was a technique we always used to cook tandoori chicken, or steak and kidney pie, or apple crumble.

While the work in the kitchen is a kind of cliff-hanging race against time of a fairly dramatic sort, involving all sorts of hazards such as very sharp knives, extremely heavy saucepans and great heat, the drama in the dining room is more a sort of comedy of manners. The dichotomy between the kitchen and the dining room is an absolute one, however, and all efforts must be made to maintain it and prevent the two spaces overlapping. Whereas the atmosphere in a restaurant kitchen is probably most accurately described by the phrase 'Oh god, this is absolutely awful', it would be terrible to be forced to apply this phrase to the dining room, where everything possible is being done to ensure that the atmosphere can be summed up as 'Isn't life marvellous?' Sometimes the waiter is aware of waves of schizophrenia lapping at the shores of his brain as he moves abruptly from 'Oh god, this is absolutely awful' to 'Isn't life marvellous?' and back again in quick succession. In the dining room, the essence of the job is to give no intimation of the truly awful amount of hectic work that goes into making everything simply marvellous.

The most difficult of all our services is brunch. Once a week on Sunday mornings, chaos comes bursting, irrepressibly, joyously and overwhelmingly into Higgins restaurant, when 150 people descend on a thirty-seater restaurant to try to eat what must be one of the best English breakfasts available in France. The problems posed by brunch may take many forms. Firstly, the place settings are very complicated: not just knives, forks and spoons, side-plates, glasses, vases of flowers, salt and pepper, but also teacups, saucers, butter-dishes, marmalade pots, milk-jugs and sugar bowls must all be on the tables. This is not too hard to have ready at the beginning of the service, which starts at half-past ten, but it is terribly difficult to re-lay when we turn round tables, which we inevitably do. Then there is the question of reservations. The restaurant is always fully booked in advance. We may have sixty reservations, which means that every table is going to be used more than once; in fact, assuming that seats will be spare at tables of three or five, some tables will be used three times. As we do not have sixty place settings, a constant stream of clean dishes needs to come out of *la plonge* (the washing-up sink). However, the main difficulty with the reservations is whether or not they will turn up on time. What are we to do if the table of four that booked for half-past ten doesn't show up until quarter-past eleven, although I have rebooked the table at twelve o'clock? (Experience has shown us that one and a half hours is generally sufficient for a brunch, especially an early one.) Or with large tables, where two people turn up on time, but the rest of their friends take an hour to arrive?

On one occasion I can remember barely being able to suppress my exasperation when a couple who had been waiting for forty-five minutes at a table of eight were finally greeted by their friends expressing surprise that they should have arrived on time for once (apparently these first-arrived were systematically late), and declaring that they had been so confident of their being late that they had decided to go to eleven o'clock mass, which only finished at quarter-past twelve, and so on. And all this without informing the poor restaurateur, who only has a small restaurant, and has to fill it up as much as possible if he's to make any money, and who hasn't got anywhere for people to wait if their table isn't ready when they arrive.

On the other hand, the same poor restaurateur, although anxiety-ridden, is quite well able to see that on a Sunday morning the mood is one of relaxation, taking things easy, not rushing to get to a restaurant on time, indeed, a mood of just lying in bed for another half hour, without even thinking that someone, somewhere, is cursing you wholeheartedly for what appears to be heinous negligence. However, it must be said that I have seldom had trouble with the reservations, since some sort of guardian angel, or perhaps the god of restauration, seems to be supervising the whole affair, and a table, even if not the one that I planned, has almost always come free at the last moment for the new arrivals. Then, on the whole, people are understanding if there is no room immediately, and offer to take a walk around the block ('*faire un petit tour*') while their table is prepared.

On one occasion, however, things did go quite badly wrong. It started with an unclear phone call at about one o'clock – we had already been fairly busy, though things had calmed down a bit and now here was someone wanting to book a table for six or perhaps ten people in twenty minutes. It was just possible. Fifteen minutes later, six people came through the door and were shown very politely to the table I had prepared for them. I was tremendously pleased they were not more numerous, since we were in fact going to the opera that afternoon, to a matinée starting at four o'clock, which meant that the restaurant had to be clear by three if we were to get out on time. Unfortunately, I had not ascertained whether the six who arrived were those who had reserved or not, and five minutes later I was horrified to see another fourteen people coming in, claiming to have rung to book and to have been told that it did not matter how numerous they were (as I said, the line was unclear). Now, I suppose, I would refuse to take them at the door, apologizing for my stupidity on the phone, but this was in the first year of the restaurant, and I could not bear the idea of fourteen people loose in Lyon, claiming that they had booked at Higgins restaurant and had been turned away at the door by the patron. It seemed to me that this would be very bad publicity. By the time I got the table seated it was after half-past one. Then, worst of all, we discovered that we hadn't enough food for them.

In the meantime, the six who had arrived earlier, and who had been perfectly served, had started to complain about the brunch. At the time there was another restaurant, called 'le Montroyal', which did brunch. Brunch at the Montroyal, they started to announce in loud voices, was much bigger, better, more varied, cheaper, in fact, superior in every way to brunch at Higgins. It seemed to me as if they had been sent by the Montroyal specifically to disrupt our service. Perhaps they had been, but with the additional fourteen people for whom there was insufficient food, the service was disrupted enough already. Poor Sue was in the kitchen struggling desperately with spitting bacon and spluttering fried eggs. I was trying to squeeze enough juice for everyone. Time was getting on. In the event, the big table was very nice: I explained the problem to them in vague terms and told them we would do what we could for them, and offered to reduce the price. We managed to serve them, clear up the restaurant and get to the opera on time, though it was an appalling rush.

On such occasions, I have felt the need to cower in the kitchen with my head in the refrigerator for some seconds before being able to go out and face the customers again, and once I can remember muttering desperately 'I don't want to go back out there, I don't want to go back out there, Oh God, I've created a monster . . .'. Still, back out I must go, and back out I do go. Generally there is no real problem that a few seconds with the head in the refrigerator cannot cure. The problem is often in the head itself, and a bit of cool dissipates it almost immediately. As Churchill said under similar circumstances, 'There's been a lot of trouble in my life, and most of it never happened.'

The real trouble with brunch is that it comes at the end of the week. Saturday night may have finished very late, but preparation for brunch begins at half-past seven: making a huge tray of kedgeree, baking a couple of hundred scones, squeezing several gallons of fruit-juice and slicing up hundreds of rashers of bacon. We are tired when we start. Nevertheless, it is a service which almost always works; less well in summer, naturally, but throughout autumn, winter and spring, we now do between 80 and 110 covers. Sometimes it annoys me that brunch works so well: why can't the other services be so full? The cooking is much more complicated, and we try so much harder with the other meals, yet brunch, basically slices of bacon and fried eggs, with only a minimum of culinary expertise involved, is what people really want. Of course, some people come back to try the restaurant in the evening, but by no means all. Some people who have been coming to brunch for years are surprised to find that the restaurant is open in the evening, having previously thought that brunch was all we did. The only time I can remember brunch being a resounding flop was the weekend the Pope came to Lyon and celebrated mass before thousands just outside the city. On that day, we had one customer for brunch and we remember him very clearly, because he ate one half of one scone of the two hundred that I had baked.

12

Of our first year's trading various incidents stick in my mind, marking stages in our gradual settling into our new life in the neighbourhood. The first of these took place in June and involved our window-cleaner. After the restaurant had been open a couple of months, I started to enquire how much various window-cleaners would charge to clean our windows regularly. I became jealous of the Commerce across the street, whose windows were cleaned every two weeks and sparkled accusingly at my own increasingly dirty ones. The current price seemed to be 120 francs a time. Then I was visited by another window-cleaner who offered to do the job for 100 francs. Naturally I accepted the lower price. He told me he only sent in his bills on a quarterly basis, and as the first quarter-day had just passed, I would receive nothing for three months. So, every two weeks, on a Wednesday afternoon, he turned up and cleaned our windows. Three months went by, and then he handed me his bill. It turned out to be precisely double what I had expected it to be. I questioned the window-cleaner, whose name I either never knew, or have effectively cancelled from my mind. He informed me that his price had been 100 francs for the outside, and another 100 francs for the inside. I asked other window-cleaners whether it was normal to quote for jobs in this way. To a man they said no.

I then sat and contemplated my windows. There are three of them, as I described earlier, and they are clearly a little complicated to clean. The windowcleaner took twenty minutes from start to finish and charged about £20, exclusive of VAT. Allowing him twenty minutes to get to his next job, this meant he was clearing £40 an hour and working say seven hours a day. £280 a day, five days a week, works out at £1400 a week, with very little in the way of expenditure on equipment or supplies. After I had finished this calculation, I decided that I was in no way rich enough to employ someone whose annual income seemed to exceed £50,000. In addition, he had broken a pane of glass in the door, which he had shown no inclination to pay for, immediately asking me if I had an insurance which would cover its loss. I do have an insurance which covers glass breakages, but does not pay the first 600 francs. Besides, since it was he who broke the window, I felt that it was his insurance which should have been called into play.

Further discussions with the window cleaner revealed that he was prepared to do the work for 150 francs. I pointed out that this was still 30 francs more than his colleagues' quotations, but he was prepared to go no further, pleading taxes, professional contributions and so on. I suggested that we should terminate our relationship and that, since there had been misunderstanding on both sides, I was prepared to pay his bill, but at the reduced level he had suggested as acceptable for the work, at the same time deducting the price of replacing the window he had broken. It was at this point that he started shouting at me. We were standing in the street outside the restaurant, and after a few seconds of shouting, I noticed the faces of a considerable number of spectators appearing in the windows up and down the street. He had discussed the question with his family, he roared, and they were a hundred per cent behind him in the matter. He had his taxes, he had his contributions to pay. Trust a foreigner to behave so unreasonably, and was I, or was I not, going to pay his bill? My repetition of my offer produced a new outburst. 'That stupid little window I broke with the tip of my toe . . .My work! Your windows! My family agrees with ME! . . . You foreigners . . .' and so on. After a while I had had enough and retreated into my alleyway, closing the door firmly, after informing him that I would see him when he was calmer.

Ten minutes later, the phone rang:

'MONSIEUR HIGGINS! JE SUIS PLUS CALME MAIN-TENANT EST-CE QUE VOUS ALLEZ ME PAYER CETTE NOTE UNE FOIS ET POUR TOUTES? SI NON . . .'. There followed a list of the terrible things that would happen if he did not receive payment, consisting mostly of visits to the restaurant with his family (still right there, behind him) to create what he referred to as '*un scandale*' so as to drive away potential trade. Eventually he calmed down enough for me to talk to him. I came downstairs, explained yet again what I was prepared to do, gave him a cheque and off he went. I still see him regularly around the Croix-Rousse; when he catches sight of me he either goes scuttling into a doorway, or adopts an air of smouldering self-righteousness.

Another incident took place around the same time that seemed in some way to be connected to the first.

Alain Ville had recommended to us a very reliable couple, Marcel and Josette Dodet, who lived in a third-floor flat just across the road and whom we approached to look after Xavier during our lunchtime services. Five days a week, Wednesday to Sunday, Xavier was taken over the road and left with M. and Mme Dodet for several hours. At night he slept upstairs in our flat, in contact with the restaurant via a house-phone. The Dodets therefore made it possible for us to operate at lunchtime, and at this early stage in our relationship, I thought very little of their obvious eccentricity.

There was, for example, the evidence of their sitting room. This rather small room was heated to sub-tropical temperatures by a large, oil-burning stove in the corner. Plants, purchased in abundance some years before, had thrived in these conditions. Vast Douanier Rousseau-like species, with thick fleshy leaves, sent tendrils crawling across the ceiling, round door and window frames, and made it difficult to sit down in certain chairs specifically designated to support trailing branches. One of the windows was permanently bound shut by some particularly muscular-looking creeper. About forty canaries, some almost totally devoid of plumage, in various cages around the room, completed the South Sea Island décor and rendered conversation impossible by the loudness of their chirping.

If the luxuriant foliage, the jungle heat and the birds were not sufficient to point to an advanced level of eccentricity, then Marcel's collection of firearms should have been a warning to us. These were produced fairly late in our friendship, with some pride. It appeared that the Dodets lived in constant fear of an armed assault mounted from the landing and bursting through their hallway, down the passageway past the sitting room, and then on further into the recesses of the apartment. To face up to such an eventuality, they had taken the necessary precautions. Their first line of defence was a starting pistol, kept permanently on a tall piece of furniture just next to the front door. If this failed, and a retreat was forced into the sitting room, then two small revolvers were conveniently placed on shelves against the wall, not too near the principal sources of jungle growth, so unlikely to be found pinned down by vegetation in cases of emergency. In the almost unforeseeable event of this second line failing, both Marcel and Josette Dodet had taken the final, no doubt sensible precaution of keeping a couple of repeater rifles under their beds, with which they could both blast away at invaders together, repelling them once and for all, though, should the worst occur, their son, Jean-François Dodet, whose room was further down the passage, was also equipped with a relatively realistic-looking cowboy pistol.

Of course, since they were all 'repliguns', none of these

weapons could actually fire bullets, but they must have been capable of producing a formidable barrage of noise. Now, you may ask, in a peaceful area of town like the Croix-Rousse, are the Dodets in any danger of attack? The answer is no. There is no earthly chance of it ever happening. The fact was, they were more or less mad. They lived in a world informed by television and the more dubious press of the 'Baker's wife shot dead for two croissants' variety, and they mistrusted or disliked everyone else in the street. They clearly felt the threat was genuine. I suppose these things should have made me at least a little sceptical of the Dodets' suitability as child-minders, but I was so relieved to have found a satisfactory way of dealing with the problem of keeping Xavier happy at midday that I didn't bother to think about it. In any case, Xavier seemed perfectly content to be with them, and they were obviously glad to have him.

Anyway, two things precipitated the downfall of our relationship with the Dodets. The first was our decision to close at lunchtime, making it no longer necessary to take Xavier over there. The second was a prolonged visit by a young woman from England, who stayed with us to perfect her French, and took charge of Xavier during our only remaining daytime service, brunch on Sundays. These two events coincided almost precisely with the window-cleaner incident. From that time on, I detected a coldness in the air when I popped over to see Marcel and Josette. Marcel would sit rapping disconsolately at the canary cages with his stick and Josette harangued me sulkily, saying that the lunchtime meal was more important than the evening meal and so on. I even detected a feeling that they took the window-cleaner's side in the public argument that had taken place in the street.

Meanwhile a curious thing had started to happen. I would come down in the morning and find that the windows of the restaurant had been pelted with tomatoes overnight. Only the bottom panes would have been touched and most of the tomatoes seemed to have fallen on the pavement in front of the façade. It first occurred to me that the window-cleaner might have sent his sons round, armed with tomatoes, in retribution for our shameful behaviour to him. But this seemed unlikely; were they such feeble lads that they could not hit the windows from across the street? I asked innumerable people. I even asked Marcel Dodet, who replied cryptically that he liked his tomatoes grilled. Finally, some young neighbours who had come to the restaurant and who live in the building next to the Dodets, but served by the same stair-well, suggested to me that I should go upstairs with them and inspect the window which looked down onto the street from Marcel Dodet's landing. This window was barred, and looked out directly on to our restaurant below. There were traces of tomatoes on the bars, and on the floor near the window. The steep trajectory would explain why the fruit had fallen at the bottom of our windows and on to the pavement in front.

Clearly the Dodets' paranoia was running at such a pitch they came to believe that the sole reason we were closing at midday was because we no longer trusted them to look after Xavier. In order to express his disapproval, even his disgust, Marcel had hit on the tomato as a means of self-expression.

Although he shouted a great deal when I accused him, the attacks miraculously ceased, and there is no doubt in my mind that Marcel was in fact the 'Mad Tomato Thrower'.

The last incident which marked the first year of operation was caused by the breakdown of our dishwashing machine. A repairman was summoned and appeared with commendable efficiency after the lunchtime service. Since the dishwasher was out of order, the kitchen was in a state of total chaos, with unwashed plates, cutlery, pots and pans covering every conceivable surface. The kitchen is very small, but the repairman was large. He had also brought an apprentice, to teach him how to mend broken dishwashers. Various tool-boxes were distributed around the place, and the dishwasher was pulled out from its normal position under *la plonge*. I tried to keep out of the way, but I confess that I am, or was, rather fascinated by the dishwasher – in those days a gleaming stainless steel box with flashing steel arms whirling round inside. Now, its beauty is somewhat faded, and prolonged contact with the machine has dimmed its attractions for me. Anyway, somehow or other, in the disorder I managed to lose the keys to the restaurant and also to our flat above. How I did so is not clear. All I know is that I had the keys before the arrival of the repairmen, but when I looked for them afterwards, they had gone.

The repairmen were telephoned. Had they, by any chance, accidentally picked up a bunch of keys that had been in the kitchen and put them in their toolboxes? They said no. Reconstructing my movements of the afternoon, I came to the conclusion that there had been a period of about two minutes when I had left the restaurant unattended, the door open, and my keys somewhere within. Had some unscrupulous person taken advantage of these few seconds to slip into the restaurant and steal the bunch of keys, so that he could return later at his leisure, letting himself in easily? If this was so, it was necessary to take immediate steps to make the restaurant secure. I was reluctant to telephone the locksmith who had installed the doors, for the simple reason that I still owed him 5000 francs. Consequently, I decided to go to the local locksmith, whose shop is 50 metres up the road. But the shop was being tended by the locksmith's wife, who knew nothing whatsoever about locks, and her husband was absent until the following day.

In the meantime, I had to make the restaurant secure, in case the burglar had planned his raid for that particular night. Our preparations were elaborate. We realized that the aim of a burglar would probably be to remove our fairly sophisticated stereo equipment. His next potential target would be an 18th-century portrait hanging in the restaurant. None of the kitchen equipment could possibly have been stolen, on account of its great weight. (Besides, with the number of restaurants going bankrupt every month in Lyon, second-hand equipment is something of a drag on the market.) As far as the wine and alcohol was concerned, all we could do was to reduce the stock held in the restaurant itself to a minimum. At the end of the evening, therefore, we removed the sound system and the portrait and carried them upstairs. Then we set to work on some traps.

A short way in from the door, just beyond the doormat, we positioned two collections of empty bottles, about six feet apart. Then we stretched about three lengths of black cotton between the two collections, securing both ends of each strand around the necks of opposite bottles. The burglar, creeping forward stealthily, would find his progress suddenly interrupted by a tremendous noise of falling glass and clattering bottles.

Next we turned our attention to the alleyway, since our burglar also had the key to that door and would undoubtedly be keen to have a look round there, too. The door is a massive wooden structure, bound with metal, which opens inwards. As a barricade, we placed our dustbin against it on the inside, and on top of the dustbin, rather precariously, since the lid was not flat, we balanced some bottles which would crash to the floor if someone attempted to push open the door. Then we retired upstairs.

One aspect which still worried us was that the insurance would be unlikely to pay for any losses where there was no sign of a break-in. In order to cope with this problem, I decided to keep a camera by the window, so that I could photograph any retreating villains as they made their getaway. Having completed these arrangements to our satisfaction, we went to sleep feeling pretty secure.

At what seemed to be the middle of the night, we were shaken from our sleep by a tremendous crashing of bottles from the alleyway. 'Oh my God!' we exclaimed, 'the burglars!' I leapt naked from my bed and jumped down the stairs from our mezzanine bedroom into the sitting-room, tore open the window and yanked fiercely at the blind to roll it upwards. The camera was completely forgotten; my sole aim was to hurl abuse as loudly and vituperatively as possible. As it turned out, the burglars were in fact the dustbin men, who, not finding our bin outside as usual, pushed at the alley door to see if it were open so they could take the rubbish. In so doing, they had dislodged the bottles balanced on top of the dustbin, and these had smashed on the stone floor. I retired slightly shamefacedly to bed.

Later that morning I went downstairs into the restaurant, reminding myself as I put the key into the lock that I must not walk into my own trap. Then I spotted a friend I had to see, and crossed the road to talk to him. Several minutes later I re-entered the restaurant and, of course, sent bottles flying all over the place. This emergency situation continued for three days, since the local locksmith consistently failed to appear. Every day I would come down to the restaurant in the morning, reminding myself of the burglar trap, and every day something would happen to me in between shutting the alley door and reaching the restaurant door – something as slight as looking up and thinking 'how blue the sky is' or 'Good heavens, there's a parking space in front of the restaurant' – and I would forget the trap and the bottles would come clattering down. Eventually the non-appearance of the local locksmith became so exasperating that I telephoned the other one, who came within a couple of hours and changed the lock free of charge, since it was almost new and could perfectly safely be used elsewhere.

Towards the end of our fifth month, June, we closed down at lunchtime. The rush to try us out had slackened, and trade for restaurants without terraces falls off in the summer anyway, so by June our trade in general had reduced. If we had been really good from the start, this might not have happened, but as it was we were inexperienced and, after the initial rush, simply had to work away at building up a steady reputation and a solid clientele. So we reduced our opening hours to five evenings a week – from Tuesday to Saturday, and brunch on Sunday morning. At the same time we decided to serve until half-past ten at night, half an hour longer than before. Sunday opening hours remained unchanged, starting at half-past ten in the morning and going on till two o'clock in the afternoon. At the time I was worried about reducing our opening hours in this way – after all, we were still on the north face of the Eiger – but now I see it was the right decision. It is far too much for two people to run a restaurant which is open lunchtime and evening, and the restaurant was too small to pay for more staff. In fact, it was not until the end of our fourth year that I employed a waiter – our first genuine employee – although I had often hired people on a daily basis to cook or serve. The restaurant acquired a cleaner relatively early on, which seemed to us a tremendous luxury.

We soldiered on through the very quiet month of July, until the totally blank month of August, when we shut up shop and set off on our *fermeture annuelle* back to England. August in Lyon, at least in our area of town, is most odd. So many people have gone that you can park wherever you please. I remember coming out into the street, dry, dusty, baking in the heat, even at eight at night, and the only person visible was a sort of stage drunk, staggering almost unrealistically along the pavement, on his way to an important rendezvous with a glass of pastis at the next bar. As an image of urban bleakness, it was almost perfect, corresponding to the mood of the owner of a near-empty restaurant. Now I find Lyon in August rather pleasant. Although it can be blisteringly hot, with tremendous thunderstorms, at the same time the town is agreeably quiet with so few people remaining, and there are many lovely swimming pools. The French, during the month of August, are all packed like sardines on the narrow little beaches along the south coast.

We run our restaurant with the stature of *'commerçant'*. *'Petit commerçant de Lyon'* has a rather derogatory ring about it, and I try not to think of myself as one, but I suppose that is what I am. (Basically this means that my business is legally in my name and I am responsible personally for its debts – another thing that I try not to think about too much.) One argument in favour of owning your own business is that you become your own boss – no one can tell you what to do, when to open or when to close. You can, wonder of wonders, take your holidays whenever you please. But in practice I find that it takes a tremendous degree of strong-mindedness to close, which the *petit commerçant de Lyon* does not always possess. In the *petit commerçant's* imagination, his entire clientele is knocking at the closed door of his restaurant, or telephoning to make a reservation, during his absence. Actually, the poor chap finds it quite tricky to relax with his head full of this kind of thing when on holiday.

As for choosing when to take a holiday, the closings of the restaurant are more or less dictated by the vagaries of the trade. There is not much point in staying open in August in our area of town, since there are really very few people about. The number of terraces in the centre of town has increased a great deal recently, with the closing of certain streets to traffic. Thus, such custom as remains in Lyon, along with the tourist trade, is very strongly concentrated in the centre of the town. August holidays are imposed on us, therefore. The month of May is punctuated by a large number of national holidays – Labour Day, European Armistice Day, the Ascension of Our Lord. Obviously, many people add these days to a Saturday and Sunday – *'faire le pont'* – and go away, or take a long weekend. So the restaurant sometimes takes a week off in May as well. Inevitably, on our return we are greeted by customers who say that they tried to come the week before, but could not, they add reproachfully, because we were closed. On the whole, though, the French understand the business of the *fermeture annuelle* or even *ponctuelle*, far better than the British would. I can think of very few establishments in London which close as we do. Perhaps their running costs are too high. But there again, there are very few restaurants in London that are run by only two or three people: there always seem to be endless staff running around. In Lyon there are innumerable small restaurants operated by the *patron* and the *patronne*. The service is more personal than it would be in Britain, where you rarely come into contact with the owners of the restaurant themselves. The French public, knowing the *patron* and *patronne* personally, understands that they occasionally need a holiday.

After seven months of trading, we shut up shop for the whole month of August and set off back to Britain for our first holiday. It was so cold in England that year that we had to buy ourselves entire new sets of clothes. Mild paranoia came on holiday with me, prompting me to ring our neighbours up from time to time, to find out whether the restaurant was still standing. Had all the customers who were ever going to come to Mister Higgins already come? Was there any point in opening up again? But it must be remembered that although food and drink bills stop when the restaurant is shut, and electricity and gas are greatly reduced, other bills keep on just the same – insurance, the loan, the rent, pension payments, social security, various taxes and so forth. The one bill that most absolutely stops is your salary. While we shivered in Britain, the imaginary phantoms of my customers reproaching me for my absence, Lyon baked under the white August heat, and the restaurant, its windows blanked out, the chairs and tables stacked neatly against the walls, and the green parquet floor beautifully polished, would, I had to keep reminding myself, be filled once again with conversation, the clatter of knives and forks on plates, the tinkle of glasses and the noise of wine pouring from a bottle, with smoke from cigarettes, smells from the kitchen, the phone ringing, music playing on the stereo – all the sounds and smells that make up our trade.

13

In my memory, our first year of business tends to resemble one of those TV shows which gathers together all the out-takes, where the presenter stumbles over his words to produce a double-entendre of seaside-postcard naughtiness, or where a particularly desirable effect, carefully sought after, repeatedly fails to work. Nowadays I have a kind of intuition about impending trouble, but at the beginning I could have done with a flashing arrow cue above the heads of potential trouble-makers, with a droning voice-over: 'Everything is going according to plan, but watch out for the customer at table number 5 . . .'.

The trouble with a restaurant is that it is a public place, and once you open your doors to the public, you may be called on to deal with some fairly odd examples. This can prompt some restaurateurs into adopting a confrontational attitude to their customers: Peter Langan famously fell into this category, but his cooking made it bearable. Who knows, perhaps his customers enjoyed being insulted? Friends of ours, who run a restaurant in Southern Spain, have developed a way of advancing towards members of the public who enter their establishment saying 'Yes? Yes please?' with intense menace in their voices. Woe betide the poor person who has come in off the street simply wanting to go to the loo, or urgently needing a telephone.

The question of choice of customers is a delicate one. On the whole the style of restaurant should dictate who you get, though clear marking of the prices on the door, to prevent any potential bargaining inside, is obviously a good idea. (This is in any case a legal requirement.) Still, I can remember at the beginning being troubled by the possibility of attracting a wide range of unsuitable customers, and indeed, one such customer was in part responsible for our first reduction in working hours, when we cut the Sunday evening service.

This service was difficult anyway, since brunch on Sunday morning was so successful that by Sunday evening we were always exhausted. Moreover, outside the fashionable restaurant areas in the centre of town, you would have to persevere for a very long time to build up a Sunday evening clientele. However, we acquired one very regular customer. He was called Henri, and even the bistro across the road assimilated him with difficulty into their clientele. He cultivated a faintly military air, based on the fact that he had been an *ancien déporté* (interned in a German prison camp) during World War II. Every now and then he would draw himself up, back more or less straight, and announce '*Ancien déporté, moi, de la guerre de trente-neuf*'. His hand would start to flicker in a faint salute, which he would think better of at the last minute, and convert into a smoothing down of his hair. In fact, he was really a seedy old roué, who had somehow or other tricked a pension out of the state so that he had never had to work, and could spend all his days playing cards in bars. Sunday evenings must have been hard for him, since most of the bars in Croix-Rousse are shut.

At all events, he took to coming to our restaurant, and after two or three visits, began to complain about the prices. Why he wanted to know, were our kirs 12 francs, when across the road they only cost 6 francs? I pointed out that ours were almost double the size and were made with far higher quality ingredients – the wine used cost about 30 francs a bottle, while across the road they used wine costing 7 francs a litre. Could we not, he asked, in view of the notable role he had played in history as an '*ancien déporté*', do a little something on the price? He smoked unfiltered French cigarettes non-stop, even puffing away between mouthfuls, the ash falling into his food. This habit would sometimes provoke terrible paroxysms of coughing, so noisy that all other conversation would cease in the room, and customers would watch in fascinated horror, as Henri ended his fit by hawking extremely loudly into his laundered, starched napkin. Passionately the anguished restaurateur wished him to be '*déporté*' on a permanent basis out of his restaurant.

Apart from Henri, who no longer bothered us after we

closed on Sunday nights, we have not really had trouble with unsuitable clients and the whole business is largely the product of restaurateur paranoia. We have shown the odd drunk to the door, especially if, once seated, he has started to make adverse comments about British cooking. However, the service was interrupted one night, when a very shambling and dishevelled figure came in through the door and made his way directly towards the kitchen, where Sue was working. I was standing at a table in the corner of the room, and called across the restaurant, instantly silencing the conversation in the room, then crossed quickly towards the man, now standing hesitantly in the middle of the floor. He mumbled something incoherent at me, as I guided him towards the door. 'No, no,' I said, 'you've got the wrong side of the street, we haven't got a bar licence here. Just cross the road and go to the Commerce.' (It's always a joy to direct unsuitable customers to other establishments.) He continued mumbling in a slightly plaintive way, but put up no resistance. I opened the door and encouraged him out into the street, pointing to my neighbours, the Commerce, who cater for a wider range of customers than us. Some minutes later, I realized that he had been muttering *'un verre d'eau, s'il vous plaît'* – 'just a glass of water, please'. I felt like I had given a fellow human being a good kick while he was lying in the gutter.

Then there was Dubois. Dubois is a very tall, intellectual-looking man who lives in the Croix-Rousse. By no means a tramp, although sometimes rather scruffy, I do not think it would be wrong to say that the light of madness shines clearly from his eyes. On one memorable visit to the restaurant he came alone but, much to the surprise of the other customers, maintained a constant stream of chatter, often commenting on the food. *'Ça, c'est de la cuisine, Ça! Mais si, je te le dis – ça, c'est de la vraie cuisine. T'as jamais goûté quelque-chose de pareil, j'imagine? Non? et alors? . . .'.* Notwithstanding the appreciative nature of his remarks, I eventually had to go over and ask him to quieten down. On leaving, he presented me with a book taken from the local library, and, as a surrealistic touch, the nameplate from a front door, inscribed 'Dubois', which is why we gave him this name.

Detailed accounts of errors and catastrophes tend to give the impression that the work is always unremittingly awful. But this is far from true: it's simply that the mistakes remain indelibly engraved in our memories. When the restaurant is going well, with people being served as quickly as they should be, the kitchen perfectly in rhythm with the room and everyone apparently enjoying themselves, then the work is unquestionably joyful. Despite the Lyonnais reputation for coldness and cliquiness, we have found our customers very open and generous in their invitations to us to visit their homes. Sometimes, being British, and even more withdrawn than the Lyonnais, we have been a little stand-offish about accepting; after all, when you have only two evenings off a week, you don't always want to spend them with people whom you see in the course of your work. Nevertheless, the evenings we have spent with customers will undoubtedly be among the most pleasant memories of having owned a restaurant when the time comes for me not to own one any more. Many have become good friends, and the restaurant is a sort of meeting place for large numbers of our neighbours, who might otherwise never have come to know each other. Not only have we been invited to customers' homes, we have been lent their cars, taken up to their flats in the mountains, shown how to ski. They have looked after Xavier for us, even taken him to the country for weekends. We have been lent a house in L'Ain for a summer holiday, with a river running at the bottom of the garden where we could swim, with crayfish hiding under the rocks of the riverbed and trout floating in the shadowy waters. I have even become a godparent to a child of some friends we met through the restaurant. Yet I suppose the nicest thing about owning a restaurant, to which all this bears witness, is that we are making our living out of doing something that gives people enjoyment, and enjoy it they must, or they wouldn't keep coming back.

One of the first lessons we learned about customer control was to beware of groups. Groups are not easy to handle in a small restaurant, and the only way to control them is to instill absolute discipline from the outset – from the phone-call making the reservation. Ideally, a fifty per cent deposit should be insisted on, in order to make sure that the group in question actually turns up: otherwise it is possible to refuse people who wanted to come to the restaurant, only to find yourself left with empty seats. Another trick which groups may hold in store for you – in some ways worse than not turning up – is turning up more numerous than their reservation. Our restaurant is limited both in space – it is impossible to make a table for more than fourteen – and in the number of chairs: we have thirty. Consequently, when the group arrives at the door and announces that, instead of twelve people, they are now sixteen, since they met up with a few friends on the way, it is not all good news as far as we are concerned. If the rest of the room is empty, then we can split the table in two. If every other seat is taken, the group, anxious to eat, having been detained in several bars before its arrival, will make helpful suggestions, such as 'we can sit on each others' knees . . .'. But this does not take into account the fact that the quantity of food may be limited – and groups who have not had a specific menu devised for them tend to play followthe-leader in their order, without bothering to look at what is on offer: 'I'll just take the same as him', 'So will I', and so on, thus unbalancing the choice of food. The reason for this is quite simple. When four people go to a specific restaurant, their main purpose is, of course, to be together: but it is also to try the restaurant, or to share it with friends, or to return to it because it was nice last time. But a group is a group for another reason and may be there because one of its members knows the restaurant and has suggested it to the others. They may be a club of wind-surfers, or 4×4 drivers, or water-colourists, or pot-holers, or hang-gliders, or Harley-Davidson enthusiasts; they are not in the restaurant for the restaurant's sake, but for the sake of their hobby. So the perfectly natural 'sheep syndrome' comes into play. As the French comedian Coluche commented, untranslatably: '*Chez un groupe il-n'y-a qu'un seul esprit – l'esprit de groupe.*'

Because our kitchen is so small, serving groups is very hard, since there is no room to put out twelve dinner plates at the same time. Then the group itself will dominate the restaurant in terms of noise generated, making it less agreeable for all the other customers, who tend to adopt pained expressions and look disparagingly at the big table. If the group displays a desire to sing, this can result in a drastic reduction in the rest of the clients. After all, the restaurant is only 30 feet long. We have now learned our lesson about groups, but not before having a few bad experiences. The first of these was when we received a large table of sixteen members of the most honourable and venerable Societé des Compagnons des Chevaliers de Tastevin du Beaujolais, or some such name. It might be imagined that these people would take a serious interest in food, and be keen to try our very good Beaujolais Villages, Brouilly or Moulin-à-Vent wines. Not a bit of it. What they wanted to do was take it in turns to drink a bottle of claret (though it might as well have been plonk) out of the spout of a tea-pot, while other members of the group sang an ancient and venerable drinking song, loudly and tunelessly, or, according to their seniority, chanted 'GLOUG – GLOUG – GLOUG – GLOUG – GLOUG – GLOUG' in a rising crescendo. Then, since some were having trouble remembering the words of the traditional Compagnons du Beaujolais song, they commandeered the restaurant menu-board, erased the menu and wrote up the words of the song instead. This particular group emptied the restaurant in a matter of minutes. They made so much noise that I could not help wondering if, even hoping that, someone might perhaps call the police. Around one o'clock I was beginning to consider slipping out to call them myself. Still, they left, as everyone must. Of course, none of them ever came back – luckily there are so many restaurants in this town that they could go on having monthly meetings of this sort for many years without ever visiting the same establishment twice.

On another occasion we had a block booking for the English-speaking Women's Club. This also was within the first few weeks of opening. Here, the organizers had asked for a menu with roast lamb, and they had specified that the lamb should be well done, in the English way, rather than rare, as the French like it. At the end of the meal, which in this instance had gone without a hitch, the group was gathering in the middle of the restaurant and chatting prior to leaving. It must have been just after midnight. I suddenly overheard someone commenting in a loud voice, in English, though by no means all of the women were English, that '*Her* husband thought it rather *overdone*, and *she* had found it too *expensive*'. I was out of the kitchen in a flash. The remark seemed to me to be doubly unjust, firstly because the group had themselves requested that the lamb should be well cooked, and secondly because they had just eaten a four-course meal with wine and coffee included for about 90 francs each, which could hardly be thought of as expensive. I decided to ignore the remark about the meat being overdone and deal only with the one concerning the price.

'Look here,' I said, 'you must understand that when a restaurant fixes its prices, it can't just take the food into account: there is the total investment to be considered – chairs, tables, knives, forks, linen, decoration – think how much all that costs the restaurateur! Obviously a place which is very nicely done up is going to be more expensive than a horrid, run-down little bistro without any toilet facilities! Have you any idea, for example, how much it cost to have this floor laid?' I paused for a moment to let my words sink in, gesticulating dramatically at our green, varnished parquet floor. It gradually dawned on me that the little group of people was looking at me in rather a strange way. Equally, Sue's pulling at my sleeve suggested that I was in the process of perpetrating a monumental gaffe. How was I to know that the woman was not commenting on the meal she had just eaten, but on an outing to that gastro-pleasure-dome, Paul Bocuse's restaurant at Collanges? I mumbled some humble conclusion to my tirade and slid off back to hide in the kitchen.

Eventually we digested all these lessons about controlling customers and groups, and nowadays we make fewer mistakes. My tongue still runs away with me occasionally, when a remark springs to mind that is so irresistibly perfect a reply to an irritating customer that I find I am unable to prevent it from popping out of my mouth. Great rudeness is not a good quality for a restaurateur and in general I manage to maintain the correct degree of reserve. On one occasion, however, I did what I still think of as a good deed in overstepping the intimacy barrier with some customers. We had a couple of clients whom I considered atypical: he had a BMW concession in a garage that he had built up himself from nothing, she had a lot of bright makeup and glitzy clothes. They were in their mid-forties – thoroughly nice, uncultured and uncultivated people. They were good customers, always spending a lot of money and obviously appreciating what they ate. One evening they turned up late for their reservation, and scarcely talking to each other. As the meal progressed, the argument got worse and worse. He became more and more intransigent, she pinker and pinker around the eyes. Eventually she stood up and rushed from the restaurant, leaving the man sitting at the table, breathing heavily and very red in the face and round the neck – rather a big neck in his case. I watched him for about five minutes, looking like a man who was never going to have anything to do with this or any other woman ever again, and entirely enclosed in his own obstinacy. I looked out the door of the restaurant and saw that she was about 200 metres up the street, blowing her nose under a street-lamp. Then I looked back at the man, still puffing away. I paused for a few seconds, then I went across to his table.

'Go on,' I said quickly, 'go and get her back – she's just up the street.' After a moment's hesitation, he left the table and headed up the road, to reappear some minutes later with the woman, still dabbing at her nose. For a second I thought that the other customers were going to applaud, but they managed to restrain themselves, even if I hadn't. The evening which had started badly ended well.

Running a restaurant is not really like beating your head against a wall – so good when you stop – though there is an element of that to it. It is more like rowing in an eight- or four-seater boat. If all the oarsmen are out of time, it is absolutely awful; but if they are all together, it is marvellous, for a while indeed, seems almost effortless. Then the fatigue begins. Only training can hold the rhythm in place once tiredness has started to attack the crew; only experience in a restaurant. But then there is the stopping. There is no doubt that stopping rowing is wonderful, and so it is with a restaurant. Never before have Sunday afternoons and evenings been so appreciated. Most people rather dread them, but not us. The idea of a quiet evening after four hours of frantic rushing – with the possibility of an English-speaking film on television (even a bad one), the prospect of a Monday spent dabbling, when almost everyone else is at work, and a trip to a restaurant on a Monday evening to sit in someone else's restaurant and be served by them – is so enticing, that it makes even brunch seem worthwhile.

14

At the beginning of our third year a television film was made about the restaurant. It was an altogether peculiar interlude in the life of Mister Higgins, but in a way it served a valuable purpose. It came at a point when we were just starting to tire of the whole business; it had lost the glamour of being new and had not yet begun to make any money. It had started to seem like very hard work for nothing. Now, suddenly, came the confirmation that what we were doing, what we had done, was not simply terrible drudgery: it was interesting and amusing enough for a documentary to be made about us. We were not just hot, bothered cooks and waiters, or damp, exhausted washers-up. We were unusual characters, called upon to provide half an hour's home entertainment for thousands of people in Britain. The whole thing renewed our self-esteem. Besides, there is scarcely a single restaurateur who does not want to get on to the telly. We all want to be up there, pushing our restaurants, telling people how to cook things and what wine to buy, and pontificating about life in general. Restaurateurs are dreadful show-offs.

Our big break for fame and fortune came about in the following way. In the second year of the restaurant we were visited by our friend Jay McDonnell. Jay, despite being submitted to a terrible regime of washing up (we scarcely let him out of the kitchen during his entire stay), was sufficiently impressed by the restaurant to speak about it in glowing terms to his brother, Steve, who works in the heady world of televison. Steve was in fact a tele-journalist for TVS based in Southampton. At that time the company was making a series of programmes which went under the general title 'Made in the South', I think. With a tremendous amount of stretching, the original idea was made to contain a programme about a 'local boy' (my parents' house in Wiltshire lies only about 20 miles outside the TVS region) going to France and setting up an English restaurant there. The programme was called 'The Horror of the English Pudding', after the story I told in the opening chapter of this book.

The director's name was Alan Ravenscroft, and it was clear from the outset that he was a man of genius. As soon as he sat down in the restaurant at the table reserved for the crew when they came to do their recce, and ordered two bottles of Saint-Véran and two bottles of Brouilly after only the most cursory of glances at the wine list, I knew that here was a man who appreciated a good restaurant when he saw one, the sort of customer dear to a restaurateur's heart. There was no careful scanning of the wine list in order to select a half bottle of the cheapest wine. Of course, there were six people at the table in all, and they were all on expenses. I had been so nervous about the restaurant being empty that night – a Saturday in December – that I had taken care to pack it a bit, and one of the tables was filled with friends. I need not have worried, however, since we were absolutely full, and refusing customers at the door. Besides, Steve told me afterwards that the crew were all so keen to come on a trip to France in the new year that even if the restaurant had been awful, they would have made a story out of it.

Thus it came to pass that in March the following year, I was flown back to England to be filmed looking as local as possible wandering around Wiltshire and eating tea at my parents' house. This was an entirely contrived sequence, since we never eat tea, or certainly never sitting around the dining-room table laden with cakes and glittering with silver to such an extent that we might all have been more comfortable in sunglasses.

The world of television seems to be very circumscribed by union rules, and certain attempts had been made to accommodate this fact. One piece of equipment that had been left behind because of these rules was a trolley for the camera, in order to do shots where the camera changes position; I think the manoeuvre is called 'tracking'. The trolley is apparently a highly strung piece of machinery and the rules state that it requires its own keeper to make sure it stays calm and under control: to reduce production costs, therefore, it was decided to do without it, and thus save an airfare and a salary. In order to replace the troublesome trolley, a wheelchair was rented from a supplier of equipment for disabled people. Apparently this is quite a common solution. The cameraman is then put into the wheelchair and wheeled around smoothly by another member of the team. Needless to say, a number of hoary old jokes about 'veteran cameraman' and 'dedication to duty overcoming a considerable handicap' were made at regular intervals. Part of the filming took place in one of the last Croix-Rousse silk workshops, and on this occasion a Lyonnais journalist was present to cover the story of a British film crew visiting the Croix-Rousse. With that extraordinary fascination that the camera has for itself, or others of its kind, a photograph was taken of the wheelchairbound cameraman filming Lyon silk production. The photo duly appeared in the local press with the caption: 'Well-known disabled cameraman essential for British film on Croix-Rousse silk production'. The restaurant was mentioned in the article, but either out of spite, or simply because he could think of nothing to say about it, the journalist managed to avoid mentioning it by name, giving the impression that it was very definitely a background to the real purpose behind the crew's visit. As it happened, the final version of the film contained no footage on silk production, which was only to provide local colour, anyway, and these images ended up on the cutting room floor.

Another scene that had been organized by me took place at Sylvain Fessy's premises in Belleville. When I rang Sylvain to ask whether it would be possible to film a tasting with him, he immediately became rather excited; rather more excited, I couldn't help thinking, than the scale of our film warranted. He began asking whether he should lay on food for the crew and so forth. I said that I had no doubt that the crew would love some food, but that he shouldn't put himself out too much since he wasn't going to get any payment out of them, and they could quite easily go and eat in a local restaurant and submit expenses to their company afterwards. He said he didn't mind, since it was going to give him some free advertising. In the event, a fantastic effort had been made. The wines were beautifully presented. A large table was laden with an immense quantity of food. Sylvain himself was looking extremely smart, with his moustache, of which he is very proud, at its most magnificent. But it was his wife whose imagination had been most inspired by the idea of cinematographic glory. The undeniably pretty Mme Fessy had adopted a costume appropriate to the role of heroine in a romantic drama, with an extraordinary, almost transparent white lace décolleté, offset with a lot of black and deep green velvet.

A considerable number of immortal images of us, and more particularly of Sue, spitting Beaujolais into a brass basin were recorded for posterity. The whole operation took about two hours. As time went by, and shot after shot was taken, it became clear that Mme Fessy was becoming increasingly restive at not being included in any of them. It was true that she had some claim to appearing, since she is by no means a passive partner in the family firm, but it seemed difficult to find a role for her to play. I mentioned to Alan that it would be diplomatic to have her take part somehow and he said that he already had something in mind. The last bit of film taken was, rather illogically, our arrival at the wine store – to be greeted by Mme Fessy in person, smiling happily at the door of the premises. It was, in 'director-speak', 'a small part, but an important one'. Unfortunately it was another part that ended up on the cutting-room floor. Even more unfortunately, Sylvain and his wife had asked for a copy of the film to be sent to Belleville, and Alan very efficiently did post one to them. Now, several years later, Mme Fessy has forgiven me, but for a long time it seemed to me that she held me personally responsible for having her cut out of the film. I still feel the need, whenever I recommend to English friends that they call in at Belleville to buy Sylvain's wines, to ask them not to mention that I have sent them, but to say that they have seen the film.

Filming continued throughout the week, working up to a climax on the Friday. We became increasingly exhausted by the need to do everything we were asked to do for the film, as well as running the restaurant, which remained open for normal business except on one night when filming took place to show how we worked in the evening. For this, all the customers had been invited, up to a point. The television company had agreed to pay for their wine and their ap-eritifs, but customers had to pay for their food. I encouraged consumption of the most expensive drinks on offer and the guests cheerfully conceded. Naturally we had invited our most faithful customers for this event, and on the whole they took it very well, though they were in fact paying for the doubtful privilege of being made to eat very slowly in a room lit with brilliant flood-lights, and to answer questions in English to the best of their ability. I had chosen customers who I thought could manage a bit of English, and some of them were astonishingly good, better, in fact, than I had ever realized. Others made charming mistakes. One of our neighbours had recently completed four years at night school studying the language. Steve, the interviewer, arrived at the table:

'What is it that makes you come to Higgins Restaurant?' he asked slowly.

'I eet lombe', came the enigmatic reply. Steve, never one to be put out by a difficult interviewee, tried another approach:

'Do you live near by?'

'Yes, good; 'ee ees goode.' Steve moved on to another table.

The following night the restaurant was open for normal business and the film crew were let loose in the town. Two members of the crew came to eat in the restaurant as customers. I was very touched. The place was full and everyone had an enjoyable evening. The rest of the crew had made the mistake of going out to another restaurant without first asking my advice, and on the last day of filming they were all unwell, except Alan ('constitution of iron – years of training, eating doner-kebabs in Greek restaurants in Notting Hill . . .').

At three o'clock on the Friday afternoon, the crew trooped out, leaving a curious vacuum behind them. For one thing, I had got used to being directed. In a certain way, it was rather restful: I didn't have to think for myself, I simply did as I was told. Even now, when I see Alan, I'm sure that if he said to me 'Tom, just go over into that corner and pretend to be studying that painting carefully, would you?', I would do it. But restaurant business soon prevailed: it was Friday night, after all; the place was full again, and life had to go on as normal. Six people had been giving us their undivided attention for several days. We had had an unwholesome exposure to the limelight, and now it was time to come back down to earth.

All in all, the incident was odd, but it served the purpose of making us look at the restaurant with new eyes, which, since our vision had become a little jaded, was no bad thing. We began to realize that Mister Higgins was indeed something quite special that a lot of people cared about, and this gave us the energy to carry on. What else we expected to get out of it, I'm not sure. At all events, the dust gently settled around the event of the film, and restaurant life went on again as normal.

The film went out on ITV's southern region and was generally considered a success. A restaurateur friend of my brother's rang him from Brighton the following day, and asked if he could speak to 'Tom Higgins' brother'. Luckily my brother is more than up to dealing with witticisms of this sort.

Lyon is an old fashioned, conservative town, much given to 'institutions', restaurants frequented simply because they have existed for years and years and have become part of the gastronomic landscape. As for Mister Higgins, it showed signs of doing slightly better. After three years people had started to grow accustomed to our faces. 'You've been here for almost a year now?' they asked sociably. If the film had gone out in France, its effect on our business would have been enormous. As it was, the power of the televisual word was not entirely negligible, since a number of customers have told me that they had seen the film while on holiday in Britain, or that relatives living over there had seen it and told them about us. For us, the most important effect of the film was unquestionably the renewal of enthusiasm that it gave us, but as far as obtaining a stardom more durable than the half-hour of 'The Horror of the English Pudding' was concerned, we appeared definitively to have flunked it.

15

In some ways owning a restaurant turns life upside down. For most people mealtimes are moments of relaxation and enjoyment: interruptions or conclusions to the working day during the week, something to do at weekends. For the restaurateur obviously this is not at all the case: our most hectic periods of work come at times when everyone else is enjoying themselves. But, as I said earlier, the most important part of running a restaurant is the preparation, the *mise en place*, and while this is not exactly *hard* work, it does take a great deal of time before each service. Thus the days become very full of working hours, even for a restaurant that is only open in the evening. There is quite simply always something to do. When you've changed the blown light-bulb in the kitchen, put the new soap in the customers'

basins, re-arranged the flowers on the tables and cleaned the doorstep, you might as well go and do the books for an hour or so, until it's time to start preparing for the evening service.

For this reason, it isn't easy to say what our life outside the restaurant is like. 'Limited' would perhaps be one way of describing it. I think this is often the case for restaurateurs. In our case, the effect is increased by the fact that we live upstairs, and so never really leave our place of work. The flat and the restaurant share a telephone number, so it is never possible to escape, except when we go away on holiday. They also share a kitchen: the flat doesn't have one, so when we are closed the restaurant is our dining room, and it is where we eat when we invite friends to come and have dinner with us. 'My,' they say, 'this is just like going out to a restaurant'. As we are clearly visible from the street, quite frequently customers try to join us, unaware that it is our day off. As we have very limited time off, if people want to come and see us, on the whole they have to come to the restaurant to do so, since we cannot go and see them. The restaurant *is* our life: everything revolves around it and indeed, everything comes to it. It is not strictly speaking necessary for us ever to go out; the fact that we don't have everything delivered is a personal choice.

Consequently, trying to squeeze extra-restaurant activities into a week filled to bursting-point with business is difficult, and can become a fearful race against time. Still, real life has to go on and work must not be allowed to dominate everything, or things would be quite inhuman. In our fourth year here, we decided to enlarge our flat, by renovating a flat we also rented on the second floor and joining it to our flat below with an internal staircase. We demolished everything in sight on the second floor, chucking the rubble out of the window, down one of those big tubes and into a skip below. Demolition is quick work, and it did not impinge too much on the restaurant. Rebuilding was another matter. We decided to replace the floor with oak parquet, retrieved from a house about to be demolished on the far side of town. The only problem was that we were responsible for doing the retrieving, and the house was to be knocked down in two days' time. This, like so much of restaurant life, really was a race against time.

I arrived at the house early the next morning, in a large rented van, with one of my longest-suffering friends. Sue had been left behind to do all the preparation for the restaurant, which was considerable, since we had been full the night before. All day we smashed and levered away, recovering not only the planks of flooring, but also the supporting joists. I needed enough floor for a room 30 feet long by 20 feet deep – a very big room indeed. The rooms we were demolishing were small, and it was difficult to visualize whether we had enough floor. At all events, we carried on working until we had filled our van, and at about quarter-past six, downed tools and ran for it. We were at least half an hour's drive from home and the evening service was worryingly close. Oak is heavy stuff, and we had perhaps overladen the vehicle by about a tonne. I just didn't feel up to driving it. The steering wheel was therefore left to my long-suffering friend, who is in fact a professional rally driver. In his defence, it must be admitted that we were absolutely exhausted, but I couldn't help feeling surprised when the first thing he did was to reverse heavily into a tree, breaking one of the van's rear lights.

I still maintain that the van was a good van, a Mercedes, I think. It was so overladen that it was hardly surprising it broke down on the way home. Luckily the rally driver is also a considerable mechanic, and he set to to remedy the fault. Less luckily, it was rush hour and the van had chosen to stop in the middle of a busy thoroughfare. As it was far too heavy to push, repairs had to be carried out in the middle of the road, with the minutes ticking desperately away till opening time. Unfortunately, at this point we were joined in our efforts by a couple of police officers, who wanted to discuss with us the business of having a van overloaded with stuff that we could in no way prove was ours, together with the finer points of being stationary in the middle of a road at half-past six, in a vehicle with defective rear lights. It looked like being a particularly nasty moment, but as soon as I explained to them that I was a restaurant owner, and that I had to get back to my restaurant which was to open in less than an hour, they became very co-operative and understanding. Lyon is a gastocracy. When we finally pulled up in front of the restaurant, Sue was leaning out of one of the flat windows: 'Hurry up,' she called, 'you're late – the restaurant's full tonight!' It was half an hour before opening-time. And that is what life outside the restaurant is like. The moment you undertake something slightly time-consuming, something a little too vaguely defined, it starts to encroach on the restaurant, and the whole business begins to become complicated. The next thing you know is that your van's broken down, and the police are asking you to help them with their enquiries.

As I said, the restaurant and the flat share a telephone number. Thus our private life can also be disturbed by early morning phone-calls. This is a shame for us, since an important part of our time off is necessarily spent in sleeping. On numerous occasions I have been called from my bed before eight in the morning to answer the phone.

'*Bonjour*,' says a piercing voice (any voice is piercing very early in the morning), '*Le restaurant Higgins?*'

'*Oui*', I reply sleepily, as yet uncertain of the time, but trying to give the impression that I'm wide awake, just in case it's ten o'clock.

'*Je voudrais des renseignements, s'il-vous-plaît,*' continues piercer. '*Quelles sont vos spécialités, et quels sont les prix de vos menus?*' By this stage I have managed to interpret my watch, and find that it is a quarter to eight. What kind of person is it that rings a restaurant at such a time to ask what food it serves? But early starts are endemic in a country which puts so much emphasis on the lunch hour. A population dedicated to spending two and a half hours eating at midday has to find the time from somewhere, and thus the country starts up earlier in the morning than Britain. The market is in place by seven o'clock in the morning. Most food shops – bakers, *charcutiers*, cheese-shops and fishmongers – are open by half-past seven, but their lunch-hour is a serious affair, which may last from half-past twelve until halfpast three. In our search to avoid being disturbed early in the morning, some years ago we took the precaution of disconnecting our doorbell, then ultimately of removing it altogether (life is so much more peaceful like that). It only took the odd, unsolicited, pre-eight o'clock visit from a representative in cleaning products to convince us that this was the right state of affairs. Other early-morning callers include the water and electricity boards, who leave hopeful messages saying that they will call to read the meters between seven and half-past eight in the morning. I have ignored these messages for some years now, and simply wait until the representatives of those companies appear at a more reasonable hour. I understand, of course, that these visits are supposed to catch the very large French working population when it is at home, and to avoid futile tolling on doorbells.

On one occasion, however, I was awoken in a different way, gradually becoming aware of a kind of ghastly, mechanical music: brainless, jigging stuff. I looked at the alarm-clock: it was before seven o'clock. Where was the noise coming from? Had I left the radio on a channel that had changed overnight? I got slowly out of bed and made my way blearily to the windows at the front of the house. The music seemed to be coming from the street. I opened the windows and the blind, and there below me was the source of the noise. Two young men were standing on the doorstep of the restaurant, their heads close together, and between them, balanced on their shoulders, a very old portable cassette player. The volume was turned up full and the music was simultaneously hideous, and hideously distorted. Every now and then, the two young men would join in the chorus loudly, out of time and, insofar as there was a tune, out of that as well. For some seconds I watched, mesmerized by this scene, then I intervened, saying loudly:

'What are you doing there?' Both men jumped, looked from left to right, then finally upwards.

'*Içi? et bien . . . on attend . . .*'.

'What *are* you waiting for?'

'*Le brunch . . .*'

'Turn off that music!'

'*C'est déjà fait.*' (Turning off the tape machine.)

'A good thing, too. Do you know what time it is?' Both men looked at their watches, then looked back up at me.

'*Sept heures.*'

'Yes, and what day?'

'*Jeudi.*'

'Correct. We do brunch on Sundays, starting at half-past ten. You have three days to wait.' It was clear that I was participating in, perhaps even ringing an end to, a memorable evening, a '*nuit blanche*'. Even as I was talking, I could imagine them repeating the story afterwards – 'He was hanging out of the window, furious, asking us the time . . .'. I suppose that if the conversation had lasted a few seconds longer, we would all have started to laugh; instead they moved slowly on. I shut the window and it was only when I was back in bed that I began to see the funny side of it. The two men were faintly familiar, as well, and lying in bed, with my memory switched on to auto-search, I suddenly recalled, from a few months before, a table of musicians from Lyon Opera, into which the two pale, upturned faces fitted. The sources of this appalling early-morning noise were two members of the Lyon National Orchestra.

However, there is one early-morning disturbance that I cannot bring myself to resent, although it wakes us almost every day: the passage of the dustbin men. It's true that they seem to delight in making as much noise as they can, shouting directions to the driver at the tops of their voices, to help him navigate the very narrow and hugely over-parked streets of the Croix-Rousse. The row that the lorry makes as it shakes the bins' contents into its innards is phenomenal as well. But the service is fantastic – the bin men come every day except Sunday and national holidays, keeping the city remarkably clean. Equally, the streets are washed every day, and the formidable mess left behind by the streetmarkets disappears as if by magic in the space of about twenty minutes. On the debit side, the bureaucracy required to keep this cleaning process going occasionally adopts a slightly hysterical attitude.

In France we have had wheelie-bins for some years. I know that we had them before they appeared in Britain, as English people were surprised when they saw them here. You can either buy or rent them; ours is rented. Almost a year after they had been installed in our area, we had an official visit from the town council to check up on the dustbin's progress. The visiting party was made up of three carefully selected men: one with very strong arms, one with very penetrating eyes and a third set apart from the others by carrying a rather magnificent clip-board and pencil. They knocked loudly on the restaurant door one afternoon, and enquired whether I had '*un bac*' or not. It was a difficult question, since the word '*bac*' is a general sort of word implying 'receptacle'. Obviously, as a restaurateur, I have quite a lot of receptacles. After a few moments' discussion, it became clear that they wanted to view the dustbin. There is a system in every area whereby a man comes round and opens all the alleyways at six o'clock in the morning, so that the bin-men can get at the bins, but my alleyway is always full of wine, so I don't want to leave it open at all.

Our bin is therefore locked away in the alleyway during the day, and wheeled out on to the pavement last thing at night. Anyway, I took the three men into our very dark alley and showed them the bin. They immediately fell into battle formation. The man with very strong arms took hold of the bin and held it at an angle. The one with the very penetrating eyes produced a torch and shone it at the bin and then read off some details in a sing-song chanting voice. The one with the clip-board entered the details on to a form. Clipboard then inspected the bin very closely, and, after a moment's conference with penetrating eyes, he turned to me and said:

'Your bin spends a lot of time outside, doesn't it?' How had he known? Was he such a formidable dustbin expert that he could tell, simply by looking at them, whether they were allowed out at night, or were kept safely locked up?

'Well,' I replied warily, 'I put it out last thing at night, and I bring it in in the morning.' Clip-board shook his head.

'I don't like it', he said. 'It worries me.'

'It worries you?' I said. 'You don't think it'll catch cold, do you?'

'I'm worried that someone will steal it.'

'Steal the bin! But no one in their right mind would steal a bin full of rubbish!'

'It has been known to happen. Couldn't you put the bin

out in the morning just before the men come, then take it in again afterwards?'

'But that would mean getting up at six in the morning just to put out the bin.'

'Yes, couldn't you do that?'

'Get up at six in the morning simply to protect my bin from being stolen by some totally loony bin thief? No, of course I couldn't; I'd rather buy one new dustbin a week than do that. Besides, loads of bins stay outside all the time; surely you don't worry about them all?'

'Yes,' said clip-board, his face creased with anxiety. 'I do.'

In spite of this very impressive level of post-installation bin-care, and rigorous control of dustbin nocturnal activities, I'm afraid I took no pity on the over-anxious bin controller. I have persisted in my daredevil ways, and leave the bin outside all night, and to this day no bin thief has shown the slightest interest in it.

In our life outside the restaurant, the thing that must rank as one of our keenest pleasures is going to other people's restaurants. Imagine the joy for us of not having to prepare, cook, serve and clear up the food we have eaten; the pleasure of just sitting in a comfortable place and waiting for an effortless meal to be brought to us – especially since we know only too well how much work has gone into the appearance of the plates on our table. I remember once reading an article about the owners of a highly successful and fashionable restaurant in New York – I believe they filled their restaurant two and a half times every night. This couple would go out to visit their colleagues' establishments early in the evening specifically so that they would see them almost empty. They derived a great deal of pleasure out of thinking that they were doing better than the others. If they really were turning over two and a half times, then they probably were, but I don't believe that this is a common trait among restaurateurs On the whole there is considerable solidarity in our ranks. I am always pleased to see other restaurant owners come to my place; if they are owners of one that I think is good, then I take it as a compliment. There is a slight element of competition in that we try to show them that however good it is in their places, it's rather better in ours, but we don't feel pleasure at seeing other restaurants empty when they should be full. On the other hand, I do feel mystified when I find myself in a restaurant which is packed out, but doesn't deserve to be.

What restaurateurs really like to talk about, apart from food and suppliers and things like that, is 'the unreasonableness of customers', or another subject might be 'the imbecility of food critics'. These are two constant sources of delight among my colleagues, and here certainly there is a degree of competitiveness: 'You think *you* had a difficult one, but wait till you hear about *this* . . .'. We are also not averse to hearing stories about disasters that have occurred in other restaurants – a small human failing, akin to, but not so pernicious as, feeling pleased when other restaurants are empty or go bankrupt. One such story which I have told to a couple of my colleagues was particularly appreciated.

Sue and I had booked a table for lunch on our wedding anniversary at a well-known establishment not too far from our own restaurant. It's one of those places that you find in France, but not really in Britain: a family business. It had been opened by the father forty years ago as a relatively humble bistro, the son had taken over at the ovens twenty years later, and now his sons were working in the room as waiters. In the intervening years a revolution had taken place in the quality of the food served: the son had proved to be a brilliant cook, and he had been sent to restaurant schools, where he had learned all about it. What had begun as a humble bistro had been transformed into a luxury restaurant — velvet chairs, heavy knives and forks, fine linen, a bewildering array of glasses and so forth. However, while the trappings of the restaurant had changed with the standard of cooking, what had not changed was the mentality of the owners, which appeared to have evolved very little since when they ran the bistro. Now, this might have amounted to charming unpretentiousness, but when you have the two sons of the house, aged about sixteen and wearing white jackets three sizes too big for them, attempting a silver service of which they are not capable, while their grandmother is ironing napkins at the back of the restaurant, it doesn't really work.

Now all this could be forgiven, even in a relatively expensive restaurant. Equally, being shown to a table next to the door didn't really matter, although our wedding anniversary is in January, and the day was cold; as we were alone in the restaurant, we simply moved to another table. The real problem arose when Sue asked the waiter if he could show her where the loo was. This request induced a great deal of shuffling and wringing of hands: 'No', he said.

'Why not?' replied.

'It's out of order.'

'And what do you suggest we do?'

'I'm just thinking . . .'

'Well, let us know what you come up with, would you?' The little waiter shuffled out in the direction of the loo, which was behind a curtained doorway, also leading to the kitchen. Then things took a sudden turn for the worse. The waiter was joined by two other people behind the curtain: the grandfather and, I'm afraid, the cook. These began to wage a major and entirely audible campaign against the broken loo.

'*Oh là-là!*' said one, '*c'est entièrement bouché . . .*'

'*C'est comme-même incroyable . . .*'

'*Qu'est-ce-qu'ils ont pu mettre là-dedans? . . .*'

'*Tiens moi ça, et tires . . .*'

'*Je n'arrive pas à le déplacer . . .*'

'*Mais putain, c'est pas possible . . .*'. Some minutes later the young man reappeared with a triumphant expression on his face:

'*Ça-y-est,*' he announced, 'we've unblocked it – but don't pull the chain . . .'

Well, the meal was a good one, and it was not really spoiled by this incident, but it has to be said that when you are sitting eating lunch, you don't really want to hear the conversation of three men struggling with the internals of the lavatory, and especially not if you strongly suspect that one of them is in fact the cook who is dishing up your meal. I can only hope that his was a purely advisory role.

16

By the time Higgins was into its fourth year, it was becoming increasingly apparent that we were going to need some help in running it. It was getting to be too much work for two people. Besides, Sue, having worked hard for over three years, was quite understandably keen to work less in the evenings – perhaps compensating by doing more preparation during the day – in order to be free at the same time as our friends not working in the restaurant business. I, as waiter, was playing a relatively social role out in the room – at least if our friends came by I could talk to them fairly easily – but Sue was shut away in the kitchen all the time, so really saw no one. Nevertheless, despite the increasing urgency of the need for staff, we approached permanent employment of a third or fourth person with some trepidation.

Some years earlier, I had had an experience which had stuck indelibly in my mind as an example of the kind of problems that might arise when more than just two people were involved in the running of a restaurant. I had gone out to eat with my brother in a ghastly restaurant in Leicester Square. It was Christmas Eve, and choice was consequently limited. At all events, we were filled with Christmas cheer, so felt up to overlooking the utter awfulness of the place. Although the room was nearly full – there must have been about two hundred people there – we were shown very quickly and efficiently to a table. The menu distracted us for a few minutes, and a waitress arrived to take our order for omelettes or sausages or whatever we had isolated as the safest bet going. Then we started to look around. Almost no one was eating. This is an ominous sign in a small restaurant, but in a restaurant that holds over 200 people, it is a sure sign that a hasty exit should be made. After a while, tempers began to fray; people are always less reasonable when they are hungry. Raised voices silenced conversation in the room. The manager divided his time between calming and reassuring the customers and rushing into the kitchen to encourage or remonstrate with the chef. And this was where the problem lay. A restaurant of that size needs five or six cooks, and here, visible through a glass compartment at the back of the room, there was quite plainly only one cook. The tension rose and rose, until finally the cook came bursting out of the kitchen into the restaurant shouting at the top of his voice:

'That's it! That's it! I've had it up to here with this place! I resign. It's rubbish anyway. I'm doing all these people a favour. I've had it. I'm off! Merry bloody Christmas to the lot of you!' And with that he made directly for the door, with the manager, the assistant manager and the head waiter running after him, their hands clasped in supplicating gestures. It was almost as though I was seeing an illustration of a joke along the lines of 'How many people does it take to run a restaurant?' Answer: 'Fifty: one cook and 49 people to beg him to stay in the kitchen.' I don't know whether he came back or not, for we also left.

Our problem was clearly one of finding the right person. Such experience of staff as we had did not make us feel confident in either our or their ability to get along together. In a restaurant it is absolutely essential that there should be understanding between the dining room and the kitchen: the work done must be the result of negotiation between the two. It is no use the dining room's suddenly deciding that the kitchen can do something – like cook single-handedly for two hundred people, or even produce a dish of scrambled eggs in mid-service – without prior consultation. Equally, the kitchen cannot take executive decisions about the dining room either. Even with only Sue and me working, things could go wrong, as for example with the incident involving the expulsion of the stray dog.

One Sunday, Sue, who is a woman of character and who is consequently capable of being rather fierce from time to time, decided suddenly, in mid-service, that we were not going to allow dogs into the restaurant any more. The decision itself was not a wrong one; the mistake was in taking it on the spur of the moment. Legally, we are not allowed to accept dogs on the premises. A health inspector could sanction a restaurant where he found dogs, but on the other hand, they don't do so, and every French restaurateur I know smiles indulgently at customers' dogs, and so do we. Quite frankly, I wasn't up to the anger it aroused in our clients when I asked them to leave their pets in their cars. They took it very personally, rather as if I had asked them to go home and wash a bit more carefully before coming to my restaurant. Brunch was particularly difficult, since many customers, having left their dogs in their flats all week while they were at work, like to exercise them on Sundays, by taking them for a drive to Higgins restaurant, then letting them rest under the table for an hour or so, or talk to other dogs which may be there.

The decision to ban all dogs had been prompted by an experience some weeks earlier, when a pudding on the dessert stand had to be thrown away because some unrestrained mutt had inspected it too closely with its tongue. The moment of its enforcement was initiated by Sue warily watching the gathering of a group of nine people outside the restaurant for brunch. This table was over half an hour late, so was already, as it were, in the wrong. A specially playful dog gambolled around their legs, and it was on this animal that Sue had her eye. Then the door opened and the dog came bounding in, with a wave of customers. Sue sortied from the kitchen and advanced towards them.

'Is this your dog?' she asked. The customers said no. Sue, who loves dogs, but takes a very firm line with disobedient examples, then seized the unruly animal by the scruff of its neck, believing it to be a stray that had wandered in off the street, and began to manhandle it out of the door just as its true owner came in with another wave of customers. Two tables had arrived at the same time – one with a dog and the other dogless. Naturally the owner was astonished to see his beloved pet being treated in this way.

'What on earth are you doing?' he asked.

'This is a stray dog,' said Sue firmly, 'and I am putting it out into the street. Anyway, we don't allow dogs in the restaurant, especially not horrid strays like this one.' I, in the meantime, having understood the problem, arrived to explain what had happened, and was bitten sharply on the hand by the enraged animal. Things then escalated in such a way that the man no longer felt able to eat in our restaurant, and left, taking his dog with him. His friends, who had perhaps had prior experience of the dog, stayed behind to eat, though something of a shadow had been cast over the service, and I could sense that we had been cast into the role of violent dog-haters.

Anyway, with Sue and me working alone in the restaurant, incidents like this one had been kept to a minimum. Over three years of running the place together had taught us each other's capabilities. We needed someone who would quickly develop the same understanding. But ideally, there was a further requirement. Since Mister Higgins does not have any particularly English features about its décor – no horse brasses, or pretty teapots or flowery wallpaper, or cottage-style furniture, the staff remain the only thing that is really English, apart from the food, and some customers question the Britishness of that, too.

So I was looking for a British person. True, we were concerned at the cost of employing someone. France is, or was, the most expensive country in Europe for employing people. On top of the salary, you must add over 50 per cent in employers' contributions to cover pension funds, social security and health insurance. But our concern at the cost was far less than our concern at finding the right person. This was someone with whom I was going to spend hours, six days a week, working in one and a half rooms together, eating together. I think of myself as easy-going, but so do an awful lot of utterly intransigent people. In the end I decided to put an ad in the main Lyon advertising magazine, which is distributed weekly to every letterbox in town, free of charge. The ad was put in for one week only, in English. We had at least fifty applicants. Many of these told me that they knew England well/had been there often on holiday/spoke English very well/had had a two-week exchange in Britain at the age of eleven. But I was after a real British person. The last person to ring in reply to the advertisement had a strong English accent when he spoke French, and he was my man. Quite aside from being British, and a trained professional to boot, he lived 500 metres down the road from the restaurant.

Thus it was that Robert Franklin came into our lives. When I interviewed him, I told him that I was looking for an accomplice rather than a waiter, and that is precisely what he became. For a year we ran the restaurant together as though it were a non-stop party, and it was Higgins' *annus mirabilis*. Robert had significantly exaggerated his ability to speak French at his interview, but it made no difference: he still managed to communicate with customers. But then, they could have been any nationality and he would have been able to communicate with them. It was not just that he was a brilliant waiter; he was, is, tremendously funny and also tremendously hardworking. I have never seen him happier than at a really busy brunch service, juggling tables in a restaurant overcrowded as a result of his policy of accepting absolutely every customer that came to the door. Somehow he managed to make this work. However, he did have some faults. For example, he was often rather the worse for drink – but 'worse' is the wrong word, since no one could actually tell except me, and frankly, Robert drunk, or hung over, was better than almost anyone else stone-cold sober. No matter how hung over, he always turned up for work on time. A more serious drawback, to manifest itself chronically later on, was a near-total inability to accept any shortcomings in his colleagues. As far as he was concerned almost all of them did have shortcomings, too. But he was expecting them to work to his standard, and no one could.

During the first year that Robert worked with us, the restaurant went so well that it was fairly common for us to refuse upwards of thirty people a night, a whole restaurant-full, simply because there was no room. Inevitably I began casting around to find ways to enlarge the premises. But there was another element which played a big role in our success in this fourth year: we had been recommended by a guide-book called *Le Petit Paumé*. This is a guide to Lyon produced by students at the fairly élite Lyon Business School. Its title roughly translates as 'Little Lost Soul', and it comes out once a year in November. Basically it tries to describe and evaluate everything of interest about the town. The judgements, forty or fifty words long, usually attempt wit, and sometimes succeed. Obviously, one of the biggest sections is about restaurants – around 300 are listed and commented on – sometimes to their regret. Considering that this guide is composed by students aged between 18 and 22, who could be excused for not being experts in culinary matters, it is almost absurdly influential. I would go so far as to say that for a restaurant like mine – small and away from the city centre – the only advertising that is of any use is either a big, fat article in a glossy magazine, like *Marie-Claire*, or a good notice in the *Petit Paumé*. So, although we try not to care, the appearance of the *Petit Paumé* each year is a tense moment for us restaurateurs, since it is capable of making or breaking a restaurant. Nor does the purchasing of advertising space ensure a reasonable article; one of the tenets of the editorial team is that the advertising department is quite separate from the critics' department, and this appears to be meticulously upheld. I, for example, have never bought any advertising at all, and have always had favourable entries; yet the *Petit Paumé* is quite capable of printing a swingeing criticism of a restaurant directly opposite a full-page two-colour advertisement for which the same establishment has paid around £2000.

From time to time restaurant owners have tried to take *Paumé* to court. There was an instance not so long ago when a well-known restaurant in town was lambasted by their *Paumé* critic as having served a *foie gras* which was less good than a product from a minor supermarket chain which was past its sell-by date. The press has its freedom, however, and if a journalist takes it into his head to write something of the sort, he can. Possibly it was true.

Anyway, since there are far too many restaurants in Lyon, the *Petit Paumé* tries to set out which are the best value, which is a reasonable aim. Of the 300 listed, some fifteen are awarded a special accolade, '*Recommendé par le Petit Paumé*'; in the book itself, these establishments are distinguished by being marked 'RPPP', and by being printed in a different colour from the rest of the entries, so that they stand out. This is what everyone wants – the RPPP. What it amounts to is a more or less total guarantee that your restaurant will be full every evening for four or five months after the appearance of the *Petit Paumé*. The effect then begins to tail off as summer approaches, by which time many people have lost their copies of the guide anyway.

The fact that we were awarded the RPPP in our fourth year of business made it even more essential for us to try and expand the premises. The restaurant had always had a problem with space, though not initially with space for customers; more because the kitchen was too small. This was now becoming critical. It was not that it was impossible to make a profit as the place was; in fact, it was beginning to treat us fairly well. The real trouble was that we had taken it as far as it would go and we felt the need to do something else.

It may sound odd, but I decided that one of my first requirements, if I was to succeed in expanding the restaurant, was more staff. They would be employed on a part-time basis initially, and could be trained by Robert, in the case of waiting staff, and by us, in the case of kitchen staff, to be ready to operate the enlarged restaurant when I had succeeded in creating it. My theory was that with extra staff helping in the restaurant, I would be freer to get together my proposals and plans for the enlargement, though obviously I had already reconnoitred at my bank, to find out if they would back the project, before embarking on a recruitment drive. My aim to reinforce the Britishness of the restaurant by employing British staff clearly limited my choice a great deal, and I had been very lucky with Robert, but we managed to find a cook who suited our requirements.

I mentioned that Robert had considerable difficulty in tolerating other members of staff whom he felt did not come up to his own level of efficiency. Unfortunately, the woman whom we employed fell into this category. Cook, whose work was perfectly satisfactory, and who sent our plates out looking far more artistic than we had been able to do, was called Wilma, short for Williamina. She had never altogether forgiven her parents for calling her Williamina, but she carried it off pretty well. Robert took it into his head to call her 'Wilms'. With his Oxfordshire accent, and a slight indistinctness of speech (increasing towards the end of the evening), the 'l' was swallowed, and the name came out sounding ominously like 'worms'. Obviously, nobody likes being called 'worms' on a regular basis, and, come to think of it, even 'Wilms' is bad enough. Since they were both British, there was never a big flare-up of tempers to defuse this unsatisfactory state of affairs, just a constant niggling as they forged a working relationship based on mistrust and antipathy. I, quickly discovering that I was a fairly incompetent manager of characters, watched the ceaseless sparring with rising alarm, as the two of them, both mean hands at the acid remark, sought the perfect expression for their mutual distaste.

I solaced myself by saying that the constant state of tension between these two members of staff would relax as soon as we added a third person. Another advertisement was put in the local paper, resulting in another fifty phone calls. Interviews were fitted into an already busy schedule. This time I specifically did not want a British person, but I did want someone who lived near the restaurant, or who had a reliable form of transport. I did not want to have to take my car and go and fetch my waiter from the other side of town because he had broken down on the way to work. First offer of the post went to a young woman called Josette, chosen almost exclusively because Wilma, who had been at work when she came to be interviewed, had said she seemed very nice. This seemed a good start; 'I can handle Robert', I said to myself, 'and I'm so easygoing, I'm bound to get on with her.'

After Josette had been with us for a few days, she started to drop details of nervous disorders and various other disturbing maladies she suffered from. No employer wants to be informed that his new employee's health is of the sort to occasion frequent absences from the workplace, nor does he want to be told about digestive problems when he is eating his supper. In her first week of work she was off sick with a heavy cold on the fourth day. There were also mistakes in her bills – bottles of wine missed off and so on. I do not feel able to practise the kind of draconian tactics used in some restaurants, where any errors in the bills are made good out of the salaries of the staff concerned. Instead I started to agonize to myself about how I was going to tell her that she was unsuitable for the job, without hurting her feelings too much. In the end I told her like this. She arrived late for work at the beginning of her second week. I took one look at her and saw that she was on the verge of an emotional crisis; having just been through one of those with cook, who was having a tricky time at home, I decided then and there that I was not having another in the restaurant for some time, unless it were mine.

'Josette,' I said 'you can see that things are very difficult for us; I'm under a lot of pressure with our expansion projects to draw up and so on, and the result is that I'm not in an easy mood at all. It's entirely my fault, but the fact is that I'm not going to be able to work with you. Now, you have a choice. You can either leave *now*, before lunch, or you can work until the end of the week.' I, least ruthless of men, had been forced into a position of ruthlessness, and I can tell you, it was not easy for me. Josette made a wise decision, and left before lunch, leaving me free to go into a corner of the restaurant for a few minutes and have that little emotional crisis I had been promising myself.

Another advertisement in the paper ultimately provided us with an excellent replacement: Brigitte, a tall blonde from Burgundy, with a wardrobe of such bewildering comprehensiveness that it seems to us that she has never, in almost four years, worn the same combination of clothes twice.

This team seemed to fit together quite satisfactorily, though no one will ever be able to anticipate my wishes with quite Robert's acuity. Towards the end of that year, around closing time at the end of a busy evening, I was in the kitchen clearing things away into the fridge. Some grapes were in a bowl on one of the work-surfaces. Robert, Wilma and Brigitte were in the kitchen with me. I absently picked up a grape, tossed it in the air, ducked beneath it, opened my mouth and, miraculously, the grape dropped in. I looked up triumphantly to see if anyone had seen. Only Robert had. He was standing at the far end of the kitchen, 15 feet from me, indicating that I should toss a grape to him. I quickly took up another one and threw it casually down, neither taking aim, nor thinking at all. Almost in slow motion the fruit, pale green against the white of the kitchen walls, arced upwards between the fridges, then started to fall towards Robert. Without moving his feet, perhaps shifting his head imperceptibly to one side, he opened his mouth and the grape dropped in. This time Wilma and Brigitte were both watching, wide-eyed. Throwing grapes around and catching them in your mouth is an absurd, childish thing to do, but the significance of the act was nonetheless clear to all of us in the kitchen. Robert, as so often, carried it off best.

'Well, Tom,' he said, 'I think we can just mark that one down to one and a half years of mutual understanding.'

At all events, the increase in staff served its purpose, and I was able to progress with my plans to enlarge the restaurant. Various possibilities were open to us. We might have been able to obtain permission to expand upwards into our flat above, but restaurants on two levels are extremely hard to serve, running up and down all the time from the kitchen to the first floor, and the height of the rooms would have meant that the stairs would be long ones. Besides, such a scheme would have given us a bigger restaurant, but also a smaller flat, and we were not especially keen on that. The real solution was of course to expand horizontally, rather than vertically, and here we thought we were lucky. Next door to us, on the corner of our crossroads, was a small, run-down bar, which changed hands three times in quick succession during the restaurant's fourth year. The total area of this place was about 25 square metres, and it was easy to join on to our existing restaurant, simply by piercing an arch through the wall. It also had the tremendous advantage of bringing a bar licence with it – a licence to sell alcohol not accompanied by a meal. I did not particularly want to do this, but such a licence adds greatly to the resale value of a restaurant. We had decided some time before that it was this premises that we needed. It would give us an extra twenty seats, taking our total up to fifty, more room in the kitchen, and also a bar. It was an exciting time for us in more ways than we had bargained for, and over the next few months we, and our new and not-so-new staff, were able to sit out in ring-side seats the final sequence of the events which ever after we were to refer to as 'The Saga of the Bar Next Door'.

17

Our street, Rue Dumenge, has the curious characteristic of not really going anywhere. This is a disadvantage from a restaurant's point of view, where frankly the most important thing of all is location. True, opposite the restaurant there is a puzzling sign pointing to the *centre ville*, but anyone seriously setting off in the direction of the sign in the hope of finding the town centre would probably get so lost in the Croix-Rousse one-way system that they might never be heard of again. From our façade to the corner of the street there is a distance of less than 5 metres, and this is the space that is filled by the very small and old-fashioned bar that, like so many very small bars in France, has the imaginative name 'Le Petit Bar'.

The last tenant of the Petit Bar of any stature, albeit a very small stature, was Albert. His tenancy more or less coincided with the opening of our restaurant and lasted into our fourth year. He was an odd, rodentlike little man of about 55. Possibly homosexual, he dyed his hair with what I always suspected of being the stuff that Dirk Bogarde used in the film *Death in Venice*. I never saw him out in the rain without an umbrella, and I suspect that the dye would have run in the same way as it did in the film, had he not carefully protected his head. Albert had sunk his life savings into the Petit Bar, had indeed sold his flat in order to purchase the business, and the business was rewarding him by going bankrupt. The remarkable thing about him was how cheerful he remained even after he had realized the catastrophic folly of his investment, and it was on this cheerfulness that his stature rested.

It is said that to be a good barman, you must be philosopher, poet, adviser, listener and drinking companion rolled into one, quite aside from being an efficient server of drinks. Albert was none of these things. The attraction he had for his few customers appeared to be that of victim. They went into his bar in order to torment him. Time and again I would observe Albert's cheery 'And how is the *jeune homme* today?' met with sullen silence on the part of the client. Then they would start to question him on the state of his business. And poor old Albert would smile and laugh and joke about it all.

In France, bars of this kind are busy from very early in the morning, when the artisans and workmen arrive for coffee or wine before work, and thus open at half-past six in the morning. But not Albert. He had tried doing the early shift, he said, and no-one came. Consequently, his hours ran from eleven o'clock to about half-past one. Then he would disappear sporadically throughout the afternoon, leaving a notice on the door saying he would be back in five minutes, and removing the outside doorhandle so nobody could get in. He would return to keep up a continuous guard from six to eight in the evening. In total, he probably attracted about twenty customers daily; some days, when trade was especially slow, rather less. The owners of the Commerce opposite mocked him for his slackness but, as Albert pointed out, why should he bother to open if there was no-one to come?

Eventually Albert decided to sell his bar. He was quite open about it: he was obliged to sell it, since he was not managing to meet the payments or to pay his suppliers. In general this is not something to be readily admitted to potential purchasers, since once they know you are gasping for money, they also know you will be prepared to capitulate on the price. For the license, the lease and, such as it was, the good will, Albert was asking £15,000. We entered into negotiations with an offer of £6000 – roughly what it was worth. This first offer was of course turned down. The weeks dragged by, and negotiations continued slowly. We went up to £9000. If these figures seem small, it should be remembered that the bar itself is pretty small, and required total structural renovation. Moreover, it had no trade at all, its two most faithful customers being a couple of extraordinary prostitutes who used Albert's telephone for their contacts.

We were therefore surprised, not to say dismayed, to hear

that Albert had clinched a deal and exchanged contracts for a sale of the business to a purchaser at £13,000. Had we made a serious mistake, we wondered? Was the bar in fact worth far more than we had estimated? Were we foolish ninnies for not snapping it up instantly?

The new purchaser was called Danovaro, and seemed to want to be referred to as Dano. He was youngish, tallish and cleanish, but no more. When asked what he had done before, he looked a bit shifty and muttered something about having had an occupational accident and got money from an industrial tribunal. Some cosmetic alterations were carried out to the bar: the outside was rendered in prickly, sandy cement, the windows painted dark brown and the walls and bar wallpapered in the pinkish beige velvety wall covering that the French love to put along the corridors of their cheaper hotels.

Danovaro then had a stroke of bad luck. Persistent police harassment of a notorious café about 300 metres up the road dislodged a thoroughly rotten group of young criminals, who then descended on the Petit Bar, and used it as their headquarters. Many of these young men and women were very expensively dressed, despite having no visible means of support, and despite sitting around in bars all day long, instead of going to work. Looking in through the window, it was possible to see the beleaguered Dano behind the bar, his shiftiness increasing by the day, accentuated by various facial tics, and a habit of rubbing desperately at his forehead with his finger-tips. No doubt all sorts of clandestine business was being transacted on his premises: small stolen goods being received, car radios, jewels, watches, stereos and drugs sold, prostitutes run and so forth. Dano must have thought almost every passer-by was a plain-clothes policeman.

The poor man was completely unstrung. Once he had encouraged these characters, he could not get rid of them, and they became his only customers. If anyone else tried to get into the bar, the atmosphere would turn to ice and the newcomer was quickly repelled. Nor were they good customers: they would sit for hours nursing a glass of lemonade or a cup of coffee. There was no cheery *bonhomie* – 'Let's all have another round, mates'. The bar was their place of work and, rather conveniently, there was somebody there who could serve them drinks, if they wanted.

Dano then made another serious mistake. He let the flat up above his bar to two of his highly dubious customers, a young couple. Scarcely a week would go by without these two having the most ferocious argument. Sometimes the bar would still be open downstairs and terrible screams and shouts would emerge from the upstairs windows. It was summer, and in the heat and stillness of the evenings, the shouting echoed up and down the street. On one occasion a television set hurtled from the window and crashed into the road below. And yet, the following day, the couple would be seen walking hand-in-hand down the street, or eating quietly in a restaurant. The man looked a rough type, though.

Time was drawing in for Danovaro and he began to look for a purchaser. This time I offered £10,000, roughly £4000 more than the place was worth, thinking it would clinch the deal. But no, someone else had offered more. And who should it be, if not the villains themselves? This was the worst thing that could possibly have happened. The bar became an abominable place. Even Albert's two customers would never have been seen in there. Fighting broke out twice a week at least – genuine fighting, with men punching and kicking each other, like in the Wild West. On several occasions I called the police, but the bar always got its shutters into position and its lights off before they arrived. One evening I met the Commissaire at a cocktail party. It was seven in the evening and he was already very drunk, which did not inspire confidence. He informed me that the bar was under close surveillance and that the net was tightening around a notorious wrongdoer who frequented the place and whose cover was to work as a taxi-driver. It would not take much longer, he assured me.

In fact, it took about another three months, during which time things went from very bad to absolutely atrocious. I met the taxi-driving suspect, whose name was Ali. I don't think I would be exaggerating in saying that Ali was a disgusting-looking man. He was bloated, dirty, unshaven. His face was shiny with perspiration, his eyes bloodshot and his hair greasy. His fingers were stained with nicotine, as were his teeth. Frankly, he looked capable of almost any crime, but with a taste for the more unpleasant sort. He summoned me to the bar one day to warn me off contacting the police when there was fighting. He told me that the streetfighters were just young boys, not used to the drink; they got excited, he said. I replied that I did not appreciate brawling outside my restaurant. He told me that the fighting took place exclusively in Rue Belfort, not in Rue Dumenge, my street, and therefore did not concern me. This was not entirely true, and besides, Rue Belfort is only a few steps away from the restaurant. He gave me to understand that if I were to telephone the police again, the façade of my restaurant would be damaged. The interview was over and I was dismissed.

Some weeks later, Sue, Xavier and I were to return to England for the christening of one of my sisters' children. For the first time ever, we were leaving the restaurant open with employees operating it. Leaving your business in other people's hands for the first time is a nerve-racking affair, like leaving a new baby for the first time with someone of insufficient experience and doubtful competence – your own parents, for example. I planned, of course, to telephone at frequent intervals, but in the event, this was not necessary, since the staff telephoned us. One evening when I had gone out for a drink with my brother-in-law and his son, Sue received a phone call from the restaurant. The waitress was ringing to say that there were terrible fumes in the room, making everyone weep. Had we used a new product on the stove and not rinsed it properly? Several tables had left, asphyxiated, cursing British cooking. Sue's answer was brief and to the point. We were 900 kilometres from Lyon. What could we be expected to do? It was up to the staff to sort out the situation themselves.

What had in fact happened was this: an argument had erupted in the Bar Next Door. At a given moment this argument had proved to revolve around issues too impor-tant to be discussed inside the bar, and the protagonists had spilled out into the street. Between fifteen and twenty of them began fighting in the middle of the road, just outside the restaurant. At the heart of the dispute were two brothers-in-law. One of them, in order to lend weight to a particular point, drew a gun and started to wave it about. The other, to underline his side of the argument, produced a can of tear-gas and began to spray it around liberally. Clouds of the stuff were sucked into the restaurant by the air extraction pulling fresh air into the room from outside, making everyone's eyes stream. The police turned up and did a great deal of standing around looking confused. In the end everyone went home. That night the restaurant did twelve covers, instead of its normal full house.

The main result of the affair was that the bar never re-opened; to this day it is still shut. I occasionally catch a glimpse of its inmates, scuttling along the Croix-Rousse pavements, or haunting other nasty little bars, no doubt up to no good. However, the fat, glistening, pockmarked and revolting Ali, taxi-driving godfather of the clan, has never reappeared.

We arrived back from Britain and were told the whole story by our very nice Tunisian neighbours who keep a corner shop opposite the Petit Bar. Within a couple of days, locksmiths had come and changed the locks on the doors. The ex-proprietors were officially evicted. It appeared that they had not been paying their rent. They had known that I had wanted to buy the place, but had responded to my offers by spreading rumours, repeated to me by our Tunisian friends, that they had attracted offers for the lease of three times the amount that I was willing to pay. (In French, the phrase 'through the grapevine' is translated by '*par le télé-phone arabe*'.) The warring couple had moved out of the flat above the bar some time earlier, and it had lately been more quietly occupied by an enormous long-distance lorrydriver, who was not there very often. He arrived back later in the week to find that his keys no longer fitted the locks. I have a clear picture of him standing on the corner, his eyes shifting slowly in disbelief from the door of the bar to the key in his hand and back again. Some of his clothes can still be seen hanging on pegs through the upstairs window. About a year later, I was offered the place again by its freehold owner, who had retrieved his property from the leaseholders by taking them to court. However, the bar licence had been lost, so the idea was far less attractive. Besides, by then we had other plans.

18

Sometimes I dream of renting all the façades of all the closed shops or commercial premises along my street and round my block, simply to enable me to put up the name 'Mister Higgins' on all of them, possibly with flashing neon arrows pointing up the street to the restaurant. However it would certainly enrage the neighbours and drive the other restaurateurs into a fury. For the last fifteen years, most of the Croix-Rousse commerce has become concentrated around the Place de la Croix-Rousse and the Grande Rue, and small shops and artisans have closed down along the back streets. The Petit Bar was not the only premises available: almost every commercial lease in my block of houses was for sale. Theoretically, it would have been possible, though perhaps inadvisable, to have taken over every one of these premises and installed the biggest restaurant in Lyon. For a brief moment, the clear sight of the recently RPPP'd restaurateur was blurred by visions of a suite of restaurants, with club-like rooms off them where people could relax over glasses of exorbitantly expensive whisky, casually ordering a second before finishing the first, retirement to these chambers freeing the tables for other clients queuing up at the door to be let in. I also envisaged billiard tables – full-sized billiard tables at that, pool, snooker, the works. In the event, we settled for one of these premises: the shop immediately behind Higgins. This was, in fact, the only possibility open to us after our failure to get hold of the Petit Bar, since the house on our other side is a private residence. We had in fact examined the shop behind some months previously, but at that time had dismissed it as too big and too run down. Now we decided to go ahead nevertheless. Well, it certainly was in poor condition. The front part had been a horrible miniature supermarket, and the back part was a series of rotting, late 19th-century store rooms. As in Higgins, everything had to be knocked down and started again, and this time we had to join two premises together. This was to be done through the kitchen.

The plan was to knock a hole through the kitchen wall, make the kitchen three times bigger than it had been, and turn what had been the store rooms into another dining room. This was to have a separate entrance, invisible from Higgins, and quite independent of it. It is possible to sit in one restaurant room and be utterly unaware of the other. For this reason, I decided to give it a different name and a different character. We called it 'Monsieur Machin (et

Moi)', which means 'Mister Whatsit (and Me)', which plays a bit on the name 'Mister Higgins', since so many people used to say that they were going to eat *chez Mister euhhh . . . Machin*.

As far as the style of the room was concerned, I suppose that I envisaged something a bit like an old French bistro: dark wood tables and a traditional tiled floor. Because the new room could not be seen from the street, but is at the back of the building and gives on to a courtyard, I thought I could make it into the sort of restaurant you discover, with an intimate feeling about it, because of being hidden away. I have always liked restaurants that surprise in this way, and I felt it would appeal to the Lyonnais as well. From an organizational point of view, a restaurant consisting of two rooms, with one on each side of a central kitchen, is a dream to operate. Two separate rooms present all sorts of possibilities, not the least of which is the ability to keep one room for groups, and leave the other for individual tables, thus avoiding the problem of noise generated by the group's table. I planned to keep Higgins' menu as it always had been, but to have a separate menu with different dishes for Machin and to move away from the more or less English dishes served in Higgins to something less recognizably national – that is, if we wanted to do Italian or French or Spanish dishes, or even a north African *tajine*, we could. As far as the staff were concerned, we would have two cooks in the kitchen – one dealing with starters and one with main courses, with one waiter or waitress on each side. It could scarcely have been more practical.

There was one considerable problem, however. Before

commencing negotiations for the Petit Bar, I had checked out my bank to find out if they would consider financing the affair, and had met with encouragement from the then assistant manager, Pierre Schneider, who had replaced the man who had supplied the loan for Mister Higgins, Jean Dufour. Unfortunately, the encouraging Schneider had in his turn taken the same upward route as his predecessor, and had been replaced by a third manager, who arrived at just about the time we were obliged to turn our attention from the Petit Bar to the vacant minisupermarket behind us. Consequently, I found myself dealing with an altogether new character, who knew nothing of me, and who was cast in a mould quite different from that of the pioneering spirits who had gone before him.

Bit by bit, the project came together. My aim on this occasion was to produce a dossier of such devastating beauty that no bank would be able to refuse it. I also felt that I could dispense with any market surveys or discussion of the competition: what I was proposing here was the urgent need for more space in order to be able to house an excess of customers that we already had. The problem that concerned me was quite simple: this time we had no money at all, and were asking for 100 per cent backing from the bank. This is precisely the sort of thing that French banks don't appreciate. Perhaps no banks do, anywhere in the world, but French banks in particular are known for lacking a spirit of enterprise, for a general reluctance to take risks unless the sum of money put forward is absolutely guaranteed. Every bit of our capital had gone into Higgins, and although it had given us a living in return, we had not been able to start saving again. On the other hand, we had five years' more experience than before; we had a working restaurant which was certainly worth more than the sum of money we were seeking to borrow; and our annual audits showed that we were in profit. The only really loose brick in the wall was the new assistant bank manager, René Brignais.

M. Brignais is an enormous man, and the office allowed him by the bank – at that time in very small premises – was tiny. It was also more or less subterranean, with light filtering in through a half-buried window. This was a shame for M. Brignais because the truth is that he simply did not fit into his office. Luckily I am a slight man, otherwise we could never both have got into the office together. As it was, the tight squeeze imposed an intimacy on the proceedings which neither of us really desired, especially not me. Moreover, I am quite certain that the closeness of the four walls around us prevented the relatively downto-earth M. Brignais from attaining that expansiveness which is the quality most sought after in bank managers as far as their clients are concerned.

M. Brignais, by no means unintelligent, has a sensitive soul which is at variance with his professional activity. He is too anxious a man to cope easily with the vagaries of trade at the small business level. It is perhaps one of the tragedies of the sensitive professional banker that his soul has to be expressed in purely numerical terms in such phrases as 'I am afraid that the bank is unable to extend your line of credit any further', or 'We cannot pass this cheque that we have received today'. Many other *commerçants* in the Croix-Rousse have found M. Brignais' soul so exasperating that they have been unable to deal with him at all. I, on the other hand, cannot help liking him, he seems to worry so much. The trouble is that he will insist on droning on to me about how I should be running my affairs, as if he knew more about catering than I do. Besides, his text is always exactly the same, and I'm now so well acquainted with it that I could quite easily join in on certain passages, or interrupt saying 'No, no, M. Brignais, you left something out there – normally you say . . .'

At all events, we got the loan. M. Brignais insists on telling me that he was against it from the start, as there was insufficient capital input on our part, but the director of the branch, M. Jules Pradin, approved it, so he was overruled. I had told them both that if they did not back me, then another bank would, since I was absolutely determined to go ahead with the scheme. In fact, despite the extreme beauty of my dossier, all the other banks I had taken it to had found it very easy to refuse. The loan came through in September, but since my dossier had on this occasion been the airiest product of my imagination, I now had to produce some real figures before we could start. What I had in fact done was to take the maximum figure I thought the new business would be able to pay, then get hold of artisans, most of whom I knew, and ask them to give me realistic-looking quotations which added up to that sum. Now I had to get real quotations to see what I could afford. We were ready to start work in December.

As always, when playing about with old buildings, things were not as easy as they had seemed on paper. Walls were thicker, thinner, higher or lower than previously assumed, and so on. But everybody has stories about renovating old houses and basically they are always the same story. Higgins re-opened, beautifully redecorated (almost no one noticed, and of those who did, several people said they liked it better with a bit of 'patina' on it), but Machin did not open for another four weeks, half-way through March. The Gulf War and the recession had already set in, but we decided to ignore such gloomy indications and, allowing any sensible feelings of caution to be dissipated by the wind, we threw the most joyous of opening parties, at which 90 bottles of Chablis and 25 kilos of Scottish smoked salmon were consumed by about 180 people. Some people drank almost nothing, and some people drank a gigantic amount. Into the latter category fell MM. Pradin and Brignais of the Banque de Lyon et de sa Région. The party started at eight o'clock. Pradin and Brignais arrived early on in the proceedings. Pradin left before eleven o'clock, smiling broadly. Always something of a mumbler, his stay at the party seemed to have increased his characteristic indistinctness of speech.

'*Monsieur Higgins*,' he said to me as he left, '*tiens à vous dire, M'sieur, ashhlurr, ashhlurraburr, ashhlurrr . . .*'

'*Merci, Monsieur Pradin*', I said, guiding him to the door.

'*Shlurr abburrishlurr . . .*', he added as an afterthought, setting slowly off down the road.

M. Brignais, on the other hand, was there to the bitter end. M. Bozzo, our fishmonger, one of the gentlest men you can imagine, took me aside as he and his wife were leaving. He had valiantly spent a considerable part of the evening talking to Pradin and Brignais. 'I know these bankers well,' he said, 'and I can tell you that ultimately, they're nothing but parasites – *ce sont que des parasites*'. His rather harsh judgement applied to the banking profession in general, and not only to my two benefactors. As the evening wore on, it became apparent that M. Brignais had as formidable a head for alcohol as he had for figures. I was personally responsible for filling his glass at least eight times throughout the evening, and I was by no means the most active distributor of wine, since I was supposed to be talking to the guests and leaving the service to others. Incredibly, his consumption of alcohol did not appear to diminish his capacity to talk sense, though some sort of inner struggle seemed to be going on in his mind, since at periodic intervals I could hear him muttering '*Je prendrai juste un dernier petit verre de cet excellent Chablis, et puis je serai obligéde rentrer chez moi.*' It was as if his better side really felt he should leave, but had decided on a policy of indulgence towards his weaker side. Some time after the Chablis had run out, he could still be heard saying, '*Une dernière petite coupe de champagne, et puis je m'en irai.*' At half-past three in the morning he was still there, showing no signs of departure. I couldn't help feeling that his wife, who was seven months pregnant, would be less indulgent than his own better side when he got home. In the end, and with a good grace, he helped us to clear up, though I did notice that as he collected the bottles left lying around, he emptied the dregs into his glass and drank them: 'It's a shame to waste such good wine,' he said; 'just a last little glass and I'll be on my way . . .'. Some days later, when I saw him again, he thanked me for the party and said that he had felt a bit tired the following day, since he'd 'very slightly exaggerated' as far as wine was concerned – he must have drunk almost a whole bottle on his own – but the real reason for his tiredness was not the alcohol, but that he had not had enough sleep, why, he must have left the party after midnight.

As always at these parties, a certain number of uninvited people wander in off the streets, and are accepted or rejected according to their appearance. This time the unwelcome non-invitee was a psychology lecturer from Grenoble University, or so he said. This man had come into the Machin bar at about half-past midnight asking if he could use the phone. Robert had been keeping an eye on the door, and showed the man to the telephone. Once next to the bar, though, he seemed to forget the phone, and asked if he could buy a drink. Robert explained that this was an opening party for a new restaurant, that we were neither a bar nor open to the general public, but that he was welcome to a glass of wine. A couple of minutes later an alarmed Robert was tugging at my sleeve, telling me that there was a mad psychology lecturer in the bar, saying that his wife had committed suicide two months before and he was thinking of doing the same thing unless things substantially improved, that probably mass suicide was the only way forward for all of us, and had we ever thought of death as the only reasonable means of putting paid to our existential problems? . . . I had one of my sudden bursts of anger. The whole thing had been such an effort – getting the loan, coordinating the craftsmen and redecorating while running Higgins, stocking Machin and organizing the party, and here was some silly man talking about suicide. It was the last straw. I went directly through to the bar and spoke to him quite firmly.

'Good evening,' I said, 'this is my restaurant you are in, this is my bar and that is my wine you are drinking. As the owner of these things, I allow myself to make a few rules, and one of these is that existential problems never, never ever come into the restaurant. Inside, everything is fine. Outside, you may perhaps wonder why you are here. Inside, the answer to "Why am I here?" is perfectly simple: because *here* is a very nice restaurant where I enjoy being. Your existential problems are outside, and you are going out *immediately* to join them.' And with that, I took him by the shoulders and propelled him very quickly through the door, shutting it firmly behind him.

Machin opened officially for business the following evening, and then every lunchtime and every evening except Sunday evenings, and all day Monday. Now, almost three years later, I still don't know whether it was a good idea or not. The work has not got any easier; in fact, it is harder than ever. What used to be a nice, relaxed, family-run restaurant, where it didn't much matter if I ran out of this dish, or that wine, has become a big place, where it is necessary to be far more professional. When I was on my own in the dining room, it was easy for me to excuse myself for not having any more of something and make a joke about it – a waiter or waitress representing me cannot do that. It's true that one of the aims in enlarging the premises was to make the restaurant less personal, and thus easier to sell, but less personal forcibly means more serious. I can no longer come out and sit with customers and have a glass of wine with them; there is quite simply too much to do.

But then, is there ever really any point in asking yourself whether this or that decision was a good one or not? Perhaps you think that it will help you know better in the future, but the chances are it won't. Some of us lead charmed lives, forever slipping effortlessly between the twin perils of Scylla and Charybdis; others are condemned to commit the same errors again and again. I'm not certain which category I belong to; I haven't lived long enough. So far, I seem to be relatively charmed.

The interior of Machin looks a bit like that of an ocean liner, with lots of dark red wood, stainless steel handrails and skirtings, and frosted portholes, so it tends to bring nautical images to mind. I often think of myself as 'battening down the hatches' when we hit a bad patch, or 'calling all hands on deck' when it's very busy. At all events, the launch of a new venture is always a sort of 'putting out to sea'. Higgins came home safely into port. Who knows, perhaps Machin will do the same?

19

Why do restaurants fascinate people so much? After all, they're just places where you go to sit and eat. Maybe you talk a bit, then you pay and go. Nothing special about that. And yet, there appears to be more to it; whenever I tell people what I do for a living, most are immediately interested and begin to ask questions about the food we serve, what the place is like, how I do this or that and where I do my shopping. I suppose it is easier for most people to ask intelligent questions about restaurants than about nuclear fission, for example, but the other thing is that running a restaurant is a job that most people who enjoy cooking, or who are fairly sociable, can imagine themselves doing. There are no very complex skills or highly specialized knowledge involved. It's not like having to be a mechanical expert to run a garage, for instance. Nevertheless, the frantic ups and downs of the business at a small scale are quite exhausting, and I confess that I am still bewildered by the fact that so many people seem to want to run their own restaurants when it is so much easier to pick up a paycheque each month doing something else. Why should anyone want a restaurant which is manifestly hard work when it's going well, and terrible when it's not? Yet people do. A friend phoned me recently and told me he was considering giving up his job at the BBC, his wife was going to abandon her post as sales director for a major publishing house, they were going to sell their beautiful home in London and buy a country hotel in France: could I advise them? And these are highly intelligent, successful people! Sue says that wanting a restaurant is a bit like wanting babies. Babies are a damn nuisance. They cry for no reason, they're ill and you don't know what's wrong, they keep you awake at night, they're expensive and they ruin your social life. But you still want them. The analogy is quite precise. Either the desire is in our genes, or love or infatuation are involved.

Much of French life turns around bistros and cafés and restaurants. The Lyonnais cartoon artist Du Bouillon frequently seeks his inspiration in these areas. A recent cartoon of his in the Lyon paper took the following form. In the first picture, a waiter and a waitress are laying a table beautifully: 'the finest linen', they murmur reverently; in the second, the knives and forks are laid in place: 'the best quality silverware, delicate mother-of-pearl handles', they intone; next, the glasses and plates; 'shining lead crystal, translucent porcelain from Limoges'. In the final picture, they turn to the door: '*Et maintenant, l'arrivée des clients . . .*' and two huge elephants come stumping in. Well, we are all restaurant customers, and not many of us are unfeeling elephants. One of my pleasures in running a res*taurant remains the fact that my customers do appreciate what I'm trying to do.

The French say '*tenir un restaurant*' or '*tenir un commerce*'. I have often found this use of the verb 'to hold' interesting. It suggests that you have to hang on to the business like grim death, or it will slip between your fingers. Indeed, hanging on to a restaurant is an absorbing activity, which does not simply involve a desire to spend one's days cooking. One has constantly to ask: Why do people come to a restaurant? What sort of food do they want to eat and in what sort of atmosphere? What can be done to make more people come? As far as we are concerned, word of mouth is the only advertising for restaurants, and for word of mouth to start working, then the balance of atmosphere with food type and quality has to be right.

The point of going out to a meal is conviviality; the food must be good, otherwise the event will be spoiled, but fundamentally it is secondary. Restaurants are a celebration of friendship, though they may also be centres of power – business deals may be arranged, policies agreed on, decisions taken. Only on rare occasions are they centres of hatred. One of my colleagues, René Lathuraz, owner of an excellent restaurant of the same name, claims once to have had a couple for their final meal together.

'*Bien, chérie,*' said the man as they sat down, '*prends ce que tu voudrais, je veux que tout soit parfait pour notre repas de séparation . . .'.* The idea of a perfect 'separation meal' is extremely cruel, and I gather that the poor woman only lasted till the *entrée,* then left in tears. I felt she was well out of the relationship, especially as the man stayed on and finished off her food as well as his own, though this may be embroidery on René's part. The most important thing we've learned about restaurants of our sort is that they are not really for talking politics in, not really for proposing marriage in, and certainly not for splitting up in. They are essentially for laughing in. The point of a restaurant like ours is to provide a background for friendship. At the risk of taking a quick dip into sentimentality, this is what makes the hard work worthwhile.

At a practical level, restaurant ownership has taught me the ability to chop vegetables very, very quickly, and allowed me to develop the doubtful skill of being able to cook about eight different things at once. Outside the sphere of a restaurant, however, this is not really very useful unless you feel that guests at a dinner party would be impressed by such an exhibition. It also requires rather more cooking space, not to mention pots and pans, than most households are able to provide, and a dedication to washing up verging on the clinically insane, since a large proportion of the dishes used will be found to lie outside the terms of reference of the average dishwasher. I have also developed an inability to produce food in small quantities, or even to gauge how much we ourselves are going to eat over a period of days. For a recent holiday in the Jura, where we had rented a house, we loaded huge quantities of food and wine into our car for a week's provisions. At the end of our holiday, a good half of the food and many bottles of wine were loaded back into the car and brought back down to Lyon. Worse still, however, is the need to go and buy food for ourselves in shops, for here two factors come into play: a deep fear of running out, prompting us to buy meat in 10 kilo loads, and horror at the price of food in the real world. Of course restaurants, since they purchase in large quantities, do buy at lower prices than the public, but prices are not really as different as all that. The real difference is the system of the monthly account. Since we pay all food bills on a monthly basis, the sum of money is so huge that the connection between it and, say, food for two people for three days, seems too tenuous to calculate. Consequently we are appalled when we have to part with real money in exchange for what appear to us to be pitiful quantities of food. What could possibly be more ridiculous than a paper bag containing three apples? Or a pre packed portion of half a pound of cheese? Or a packet of four lamb chops?

Another thing I have learned is that there is a definite 'restaurateur look', and I have got it. I think I must have acquired it early on in my career, since my trips across other restaurants in search of the loo have long been punctuated by people trying to catch my eye, gesturing and calling 'waiter'. On an early occasion, I recall being distinctly pleased at what I considered to be the flattering attention being paid to me by two pretty young women who smiled and waved to me as I crossed the dining room, and their touching looks of disappointment as I guided myself towards the loo, instead of joining them at their table. Once inside the calming, watery surroundings of the toilets, I realized that we had both been mistaken.

The most notable example of this confusion took place in a restaurant in London and concerned the same Sicilian waiter who had been ridiculed by boorish customers for speaking poor English and so forth, whom I spoke of earlier; the incident took place on the same evening. At another table were two Middle Eastern or North Indian business-men, accompanied by two women who, I had noted without really thinking about it, were hostesses. They left the restaurant only a minute or two before us and, just as we were getting up to leave, there was some shouting from outside the door and one of the men came bursting back in:

'The man who touched my woman – I will kill him! Let him come outside this instant and I will show him. No man touches my woman and gets away with it!' None of the waiters moved. 'It was him!' shouted the man, indicating the Sicilian waiter who had served us. 'Let him come outside at once now, and I will kill him.' The little group of waiters huddled closer together, and I'm afraid to say that one of them picked up a bottle by the neck and started to weigh it menacingly in his hands. I, having just stood up, was directly facing the irate man; was, in fact, between him and the waiters. After a moment's reflection I decided to talk to him, appealing directly to his baser instincts.

'Look,' I said, 'you must understand that these people are Sicilians. They're not civilized, like you or me, but highly dangerous. I should just let the whole thing drop, if I were you.'

'Let him come outside straight now,' shouted the man, his syntax becoming slightly eccentric as his passion rose, 'and I will show him what becomes of the man who touches my woman.'

'Look,' I said, trying again, 'We've all had a nice evening; why don't you just go home and forget about it?' He turned and looked me in the eye.

'Now look here,' he said, 'it is not with *you* that I am having my argument, but with your *staff*.' At this point Sue took me firmly by the arm and guided me out. The problems of our own restaurant, nearly 600 miles away, were enough for us; we did not need to stay and solve someone else's.

So, here we are after eight years of restaurant ownership in Lyon. From a converted workshop seating thirty people, we have now progressed to a kind of two-tier restaurant with over sixty seats, a small terrace in a courtyard and even a sort of summer-house on the far side of the terrace which can be used on warm summer nights. One project which looks likely to see the light of day before long is the conversion of a three-bedroom flat above Machin into a club for restaurant customers. I have taken a mental vow that I am never going to play around with major transformations of old commercial premises any more – antique buildings contain too many surprises of an expensive sort. No doubt this vow will hold true until the next time, and I confess that I am still haunted by the Petit Bar premises, which would complete the restaurant.

I have often mentioned how literal-minded the French are, and only the other night we had a particularly exasperating example of this, as I showed some customers to the door of Higgins at the end of a meal apparently thoroughly enjoyed. I told them that I'd opened another restaurant next door, where I served different food.

'*Ah*', said one man, '*Quel genre de cuisine pratiquez-vous là-bas?*'

'Good cooking', I quipped back, hoping to avoid a long recital of the menus.

'*La française, alors*', he replied, without even thinking. The attitude always remains the same: if it's good it must be French. But I have learned to adopt a stoical attitude to remarks which could, in a less favourable light, be seen to be attacking my last eight years' work. Comments of the sort are not worth worrying about. The way to stay sane in the restaurant trade is simply to relax, not to take everything the customers say too seriously. What could it all possibly matter, anyway? Lyon is a beautiful city, set in beautiful countryside; it has countless advantages, and I feel tremendously lucky to be living and working here. When things get too much in the restaurant, we can leave, and go and lie in our orchard in the Beaujolais, or climb a mountain.

Not so very long ago, we started learning how to ski. We have some friends who have a flat at Courchevel, a very exclusive ski resort. Since we are beginners, our friends let us practise on our own in the mornings, and we all skied together in the afternoons, or, more correctly, our friends spent their afternoons helping us to stand up again. On one particular morning, Sue, Xavier and I set off for the *téléphériques* to take us up to the ski centre so we could book in for lessons. To our dismay, when we got to the top of the cable-car run and got out, we found that we had boarded the wrong *téléphérique* and were in fact near the summit of the mountain, a thousand feet above the ski centre, visible in the sunshine far below. Well, the initial part of the descent didn't look too difficult, so we set off slowly, falling at regular intervals. I skied with Xavier between my legs, or tried to. Things were coming along not too badly, and we must have left the telecabins about 500 metres behind us, when we came out onto a broad plain of white snow to our right, and what seemed to us to be a near vertical descent to our left. This was the blackest of black pistes. Naturally, we paused to consider what to do, while not going too close to the edge. Olympicstandard skiers swooped past us on all sides, and I tried to look dignified as I wiped the snow they sprayed up out of my eyes. Meanwhile, we had managed to communicate our fear to Xavier, who began to cry. The fact was that neither parent was capable of skiing this piste, and Xavier even less so. We were stuck three-quarters of the way up a mountain, but were too far from the telecabins to consider going back. Eventually, I spoke to a very competent looking skier who had stopped at the top of this vertiginous descent to rest, and he agreed to ski down with Xavier on his shoulders. I was to attempt the slope carrying Xavier's skis and sticks and this man's sticks as well, since he had to hold on to Xavier and would not be able to use them. Sue started to ski slowly down, and I followed. After about a hundred metres, it became clear that I was likely to injure myself quite badly with the additional skis and sticks that I was carrying, so I decided to take off my skis and walk down.

It really was tremendously steep, and I was now quite

heavily burdened as I started to slither and slide down clumsily. Unfortunately, there was a chair lift running just above me, and numerous people were unable to refrain from making ironic comments about me as they floated past. As I stumbled down, sometimes upright, sometimes on my bottom, I couldn't help reflecting that these comments resembled remarks made about the restaurant when we first opened, and sprang indeed from the same kind of sense of humour that led the regulars in the Café du Commerce to place bets regarding our survival. In fact, the whole episode, from our accidental choice of the wrong *téléphérique* to my slow and bumpy progress, began to seem like an allegory of our careers as restaurateurs – with the advantage of several years' hindsight. We opened up a restaurant largely unaware of the difficulties and pitfalls of restaurant ownership in France – something of a 'black piste' if ever there was one – and though we may have slipped from time to time, stumbled here and there, we've always managed to regain our footing one way or another. I might also add that, in spite of such an inauspicious start to our winter sports career, we are all now adequate, if not excellent, skiers.

A
Dozen of
Mr. Higgins'
Favourite
Recipes

CREAM OF MUSHROOM SOUP
(serves 4)

We have made complicated and exotic soups in the restaurant, but this one still remains my favourite. I like it to be as smooth as possible, but if you prefer a more grainy texture, just reduce the whizzing seconds in the food processor.

1 medium onion, given a medium chopping	3 ½ cups light chicken stock (or water)
1 ½ lb mushrooms, cleaned and sliced	⅓ cup crème fraîche
3 Tb plus 1 tsp butter	2 Tb medium sherry
2 Tb plain flour	salt and pepper
	chopped chives

Melt the butter in a heavy-bottomed pan, and sweat the onions for five minutes or until glazed and softened. Add the mushrooms and continue to cook with the lid on until they are softened too (about 10 minutes). Stir the flour in well and carry on cooking and stirring for a couple of minutes to cook out the taste of the flour. Pour in the stock or water, still stirring (if your arm is getting tired by now, don't worry, the end is in sight). Cover the pan, bring to the boil and reduce to a gentle simmer for twenty minutes. Check that the vegetables are quite soft, then remove from the heat and liquidize in food processor. Return the soup to the pan, stir in the cream and sherry, season to taste and reheat gently. Serve in warmed bowls garnished with chopped chives.

SMOKED HADDOCK TERRINE
(serves 8)

²/₃ lb smoked haddock fillets
9 oz white fish fillets
  (cod, haddock, hake, etc.)
3 large eggs
1 Tb lemon juice
¹/₃ cup plus 1 Tb dry white
  wine

9 oz crème fraîche or
  1 cup plus 1¹/₄ Tb
  heavy cream
chive mayonnaise
generous grating of
  nutmeg

Chop the white fish and flake the smoked haddock; place both in the bowl of a food processor with the cutting blade installed. Whiz this up at high speed with the lemon juice and the nutmeg until it is reduced to a thick paste. Add the white wine, still whizzing, to mix in. In a bowl, beat the three eggs, then add this gradually to the fish mixture in the processor until it is fully incorporated. Finally, add the cream, using the food processor more tactfully, or the cream will begin to turn to butter. Season with pepper, but taste for salt, as the haddock may contain enough already. Line a well-buttered, 1¹/₂ qt terrine with greaseproof paper or tin foil along the bottom and up the ends (to help turn out the terrine afterwards), pour the mixture in, cover with buttered foil and bake in a preheated moderate oven at 350° for 1 hour, or until firm to the touch – cooking time depends on individual ovens. Let the terrine cool for twenty minutes, then turn out after loosening by tugging on the lining, and serve hot, warm or cold with chive mayonnaise and salad. Dedicate a couple of minutes to marvelling at the splendour of your food processor.

Spotted Dick, S'il Vous Plait

HIGGINS STILTON SALAD

Stilton cheese
salad greens
walnuts
red apples

tomatoes and parsley
for garnish
walnut oil and mustard
vinaigrette

Stilton is a delicious, blue veined cheese made from cows' milk in Derbyshire – combine it with walnuts and apples and a varied selection of salad greens, and make a vinaigrette dressing with a good dose of mustard and some walnut oil for flavour, and you have a marvellous salad.

Wash and trim the salad greens and toss them in the vinaigrette dressing; arrange them on individual plates, trying to build a tower of salad – go for volume rather than surface area – or place the salad in a large serving bowl. Allow 3 Tb plus 1 tsp of Stilton per person as a starter, more as a main course salad, and crumble this into each plate or into the bowl. Roughly crush two or three walnut halves per person on top. In the restaurant we try to find nice, firm red-skinned apples, which we cut in very thin slices and arrange in three fanciful fans around the edge of the plate – but we are serving food in the land of gastro-art. We decorate with finely diced tomato jewels, and chopped parsley.

MEATLOAF EN CROUTE
(serves 8)

For the pastry:

1 cup plain flour

$^1/_2$ tsp salt

$^1/_3$ cup chilled unsalted butter

2 to 3 Tb cold water,
more as needed

For the meatloaf:

2 lb ground lean pork

1 medium onion,
finely chopped

2 Tb finely chopped parsley

1 clove finely chopped garlic

3 oz grated cheddar
(or similar) cheese

About 8 mushrooms,
finely sliced

1 egg, beaten

$^2/_3$ cup strong beef stock

mustard parsley butter

salt and pepper

First the pastry: sift the flour and salt into a bowl. Cut the butter in small pieces and mix with your finger-tips until the mixture resembles coarse breadcrumbs. Add the water and "cut" the mixture together with a metal spoon, then gather with your fingers and knead gently – remember, you never knead pastry desperately, you only knead it slightly. Wrap the ball of pastry in cling film and put it in the fridge. Remove and let stand $^1/_2$ hour before using.

In a large bowl, mix together the pork, onion, parsley and garlic. Add the beaten egg and stock. Season with salt (sparingly, since the stock is already salty) and pepper and mix well. Half fill a 1$^1/_2$ qt terrine with the meat mixture, sprinkle first with the cheese, then with the mushrooms, then add the rest of the meat. Cover with foil, then bake in a warm oven (350°) in a *bain marie* for 1 hour. Let cool overnight.

Roll the pastry out thinly and seal it around the cold, unmoulded loaf. Glaze with beaten egg and bake in a 450° oven for 15 minutes to crisp the pastry, then reduce the heat to 375° and cook for a further 1/2 hour.

Serve hot in slices, with mustard and parsley butter.

LANCASHIRE HOT POT
(serves 4–6)

1²/₃ lb. leg or shoulder of lamb, trimmed and cut into 1 inch cubes

1 large carrot, 1 medium onion and 2 sticks celery, finely diced

2 bay leaves

2 Tb pearl barley

oil for frying

2¹/₄ lb potatoes, peeled and finely sliced into discs

3 Tb plus 1 tsp butter

This is a hearty country recipe, which can make meat go a long way. The quantities given are enough for four big eaters, or six lighter appetites.

Working in batches, quickly brown the cubes of lamb in oil in a hot frying pan. Season with ground pepper at this stage. In a saucepan large enough to hold all the ingredients easily (except the potatoes), heat a little more oil and cook the diced vegetables until just beginning to colour. Add the browned meat and the bay leaves and turn with a wooden spoon until the mixture starts to sizzle. Put enough water in the pan almost to cover the meat, add the pearl barley and bring the pan to the boil. Reduce the heat and cook covered for 30 minutes, then season with salt and more pepper if needs be.

Put the mixture into a deep baking tray or casserole and cover with salted and peppered layers of sliced potato up to the top of the receptacle. Dot the surface with the butter and bake 15 minutes in a preheated, warm oven (400°), then reduce the heat and bake a further 45 minutes at a lower heat (350°), or until the potato is golden on top and soft all the way through.

Spotted Dick, S'il Vous Plait

LAMB ROGANJOSH
(serves 4)
Indian Lamb with Almonds

1²/₃ lb leg of lamb, trimmed
and chopped into 1 inch
cubes

2 medium onions,
finely chopped

2 whole cloves of garlic, leave
the last layer of outer skin

4 bay leaves

5 cloves

8 green cardamon seeds

1 small stick of cinnamon

¹/₂ tsp ground cumin

1 tsp ground coriander

¹/₂ tsp turmeric powder

¹/₂ tsp (or more, some like it
hot) hot chili powder

a good handful finely
chopped fresh coriander

1 tomato, roughly chopped

³/₄ cup plus 2 Tb fresh plain
yoghurt

¹/₃ cup ground blanched
almonds

oil for cooking

salt and pepper

Don't be put off by the long list of ingredients – this is a marvellous, butter and cream-free dish that is easy to make, very foreign tasting and, better still, you don't need to brown the meat. Heat the oil in a large pan; add the onions and cook quite fiercely for some minutes to turn them golden brown. Next add the garlic, bay leaves, cardamons and the cinnamon and continue cooking on a lower heat for a few minutes. Then add the powdered spices and the ground almonds, stirring them in well. Finally, mix in the chopped tomato and the yoghurt, which will make the pan sizzle. Make sure all the ingredients are properly amalgamated, then simply toss in the meat, stir well, cover and cook gently for about an hour, or until the meat is tender. Stir occasionally to prevent sticking.

SALMON GRATIN
(serves 4)

For the fish stock:

1 lb fish trimmings	$^1/_2$ onion
(from the fish monger)	1 stick celery
$2^1/_3$ cup water	1 bay leaf
$^1/_3$ cup white wine	sea salt and 8 whole
a few parsley stems	peppercorns

Put all the ingredients in a large pan, bring to the boil and simmer lidless for 20 minutes. Strain and reserve the stock.

$1^2/_3$ lb fillet of salmon cut into	$^1/_2$ tsp curry powder
as many thin slices as you can	$^1/_2$ tsp turmeric
– as for smoked salmon	tomato and parsley for
$1^1/_2$ cups fish stock	garnish
$^2/_3$ cup crème fraîche or	salt and pepper
heavy cream	

This is a wonderful, simple recipe, but you need a very hot grill and some heat-resistant plates. Reduce the fish stock to a quarter of its original volume. Add the curry powder and turmeric and whisk to make sure they have dissolved. Whisk in the cream on low heat and cook until the sauce has well thickened – several minutes. Do not let boil or the cream will curdle. Season with salt and pepper and let cool – the sauce can be prepared in advance. Arrange slices of salmon to cover each of the heat-proof plates, and heat your grill to its highest heat. Spread a good quantity of the sauce over most of the surface of the salmon, in a circle, and put the plates one by one, or two by two, under the grill, until the sauce bubbles and starts to turn golden. Garnish with diced tomato jewels and chopped parsley and serve with the hot plates on slightly larger room temperature ones.

POACHED COD WITH HERB SAUCE
(serves 4)

Those who fear cream, butter and eggs, abstain from this recipe, and opt for Lamb Roganjosh . . .

4 pieces of cod fillet, 9 oz each

For the sauce

1 cup dry white wine
1 Tb white vinegar
1 shallot, very finely chopped
$^{1}/_{3}$ cup plus 1 Tb butter
1 egg yolk
a very little butter for
   cooking
3 Tb plus 1 tsp heavy cream

6 leaves each of basil,
   tarragon, dillweed, 3 leaves
   mint, and a small handful
   of parsley (preserve four
   stems) all finely chopped
   together
$^{1}/_{2}$ lemon, $^{1}/_{2}$ tomato,
   $^{1}/_{2}$ onion, $^{1}/_{2}$ carrot

In a thick—bottomed saucepan, sweat the chopped shallot in a very little butter until glazed and softened, but not coloured. Add the white wine and vinegar and boil rapidly uncovered until reduced to a quarter of its original volume. Let this cool to tepid, then beat in the egg yolk with a small balloon whisk, while melting the butter in a second pan. Gradually whisk in the slightly cooled, melted butter, over a very gentle heat – too much heat will make the sauce curdle. When the butter is incorporated and the sauce has thickened, add the cream, still whisking, season with salt and pepper and stir in the chopped herbs and keep the sauce warm while you cook the fish.

For the bouillon, fill a three inch deep, rectangular metal baking tray, large enough to hold the four pieces of fish, almost to the brim with water. If you feel rich, replace some of the water with a half pint of white wine. Then add half a lemon, half an onion, half a tomato, the reserved parsley stems, eight peppercorns, two teaspoons of salt and a bit of peeled carrot. Bring to the boil on top of the stove, then let simmer gently. Place the fish fillets in the simmering bouillon, and let them bubble gently for 3 to 5 minutes, depending on their thickness – the flesh should feel soft and be just beginning to flake. Remove them with a slotted spatula, drain them and put them on warmed plates – cover with the sauce.

STEAK AND KIDNEY PIE
(Serves 4)

Although traditionally a pale dish, I prefer my meat mixture to be sealed before baking – making it a rich brown colour.

Pastry (see Meatloaf recipe)
$^1/_2$ lb ox kidney, trimmed and diced into medium bite-sized pieces
$1^1/_2$ lb stewing steak, trimmed and cut into 1 inch cubes

1 medium onion chopped finely
2 bay leaves
oil for frying
seasoned flour
beaten egg for glazing pastry
salt and pepper

Heat the oil in a large saucepan and cook the onion until it starts to turn golden. Toss all the meat in a dish of flour seasoned with salt and pepper, then add this to the onion, and brown the meat on all sides, raising the heat if necessary. If your pan is not a good, big pan, you may need to brown the meat separately in a frying pan. Add the bay leaves and stir constantly while pouring in enough water almost to cover the meat. Bring the mixture to a boil, then reduce the heat and simmer, covered, until the meat is tender – this may take $1^1/_2$ to 2 hours, depending on the cut of meat you use. Adjust the seasoning and let the mixture cool. Put the mixture into a 9–10″ deep pie dish, roll out the same type of pastry as for meatloaf, and cover the dish with it, crimping the edges and decorating with flowers and leaves as you wish. Glaze with beaten egg and bake in a pre-heated oven for 15 minutes at 400° to brown the pastry, then reduce the heat and cook for a further 30 minutes at 350°.

Spotted Dick, S'il Vous Plait

TRIFLE

The cake:

2 whole eggs	1 pinch salt
¹/₃ cup fine granulated sugar	4–5 oz madeira or medium
¹/₃ cup plus 3 Tb plain flour	sherry
1 scant tsp baking powder	

In a mixer, beat together the eggs and the sugar until they thicken and whiten. Sift together the dry ingredients and fold into the egg mixture. Scrape into a buttered 8-inch cake tin and bake in a preheated, moderate oven (375°) for 15 minutes, or until well risen and firm in the centre. Let cool, then break roughly into the bottom of a large glass bowl. Sprinkle with the madeira or sherry.

The custard:

1 cup milk	3 egg yolks
1 cup heavy cream	a few drops vanilla
¹/₃ cup plus 1 Tb fine	4 fine leaves or 1 Tb
granulated sugar	powdered gelatine

Heat the milk and cream together to boiling point, add the vanilla essence. Whisk the egg yolks and the sugar together until they whiten and thicken. Pour the hot liquid over the egg mixture stirring all the time – return this to the pan and cook very gently, stirring continuously until it starts to thicken and attain the peculiar status of being able to coat the back of a wooden spoon. Soften the gelatine in a bowl of cold water, wring it out and stir it into the hot custard. Set aside to cool.

The rest:

1 ¹/₂ pt strawberries	²/₃ cup plus 2 Tb
1 ¹/₂ pt raspberries	whipping cream
3 Tb plus 1 tsp	3 Tb plus 1 tsp confectioners
sugar	sugar

Hull and wash the strawberries and chop them onto the cake in the bowl. Rinse the raspberries (if they need it) and scatter over the strawberries; sprinkle with sugar. When the custard is beginning to set, pour it over the fruit, cover the dish with cling film and put it into what my mother still refers to as the 'ice chest'. Whip the cream stiffly with the confectioners sugar and before serving, spread this final layer over the top of the pudding. Decorate, if you wish, with angelica, candied fruit and sweet almonds.

IRISH COFFEE MOUSSE

4 eggs, yolks and whites separated	5 fine leaves or 2 tsp powdered gelatine
¹/₃ cup sugar	¹/₃ cup plus 1 Tb Irish whiskey
³/₄ cup hot black coffee	Irish whiskey
²/₃ cup plus 2 Tb whipping cream, well chilled	chocolate sauce

Beat the egg yolks with the sugar in a round—bottomed bowl until the mixture whitens and thickens. Pour in the hot coffee, stirring all the time. Set the bowl containing this mixture over a saucepan holding simmering water. The pan should be just smaller than the bowl in circumference, so as to hold it without its bottom touching the water. Stir constantly with a wooden spoon until the coffee custard thickens. Remove and cool.

Soak the gelatine in cold water until soft. Heat the whiskey till it steams – ignite the fumes if you wish to burn off the alcohol. Wring out the gelatine well and stir it into the whiskey. Leave to cool to a tepid fluid.

Beat the cream and the egg white in their separate bowls to soft peaks, then stir the whiskey into the coffee custard, which should not be cold from the fridge, but absolutely cool nonetheless. Then, first fold in the whipped cream – if the temperature is cool enough, the mixture should begin to thicken more, and 'take'. Then fold in the beaten egg whites, using a metal spoon or spatula. Pour into a glass serving bowl, cover with cling film and put into the fridge. Serve with a warm chocolate sauce.

SPOTTED DICK

1 cup self-rising flour	pinch of salt
1/2 cup beef suet,	4 Tb sultanas
chopped very fine	2 Tb currants
4 Tb white sugar	4 Tb raisins
1 egg, beaten	2 Tb chopped dates
milk to mix	1 Tb golden syrup

Sift the flour and salt into a mixing bowl. Stir in the suet with a wooden spoon. Add the sugar and dried fruit, still stirring. Mix in the egg and enough milk to obtain a soft dropping consistency. Add the syrup. Scrape into a well-buttered 2 pint pudding basin. Cover first with a large piece of buttered parchment paper. Then cover with a sheet of foil. Cut a generous overlap around the basin, bend this down and fasten very tightly with a double string below the lip of the basin to seal the water out. You may need help to do this. Cook the pudding in a steamer for 1 1/4 hours. Pudding should be firm. Turn the pudding out and serve with custard (use recipe for trifle custard without the gelatine.)

This is a dessert that has been served to generations of schoolboys and girls, as well as to the armed forces. The Higgins recipe comes courtesy of a friend, Susan Al-Khatib.